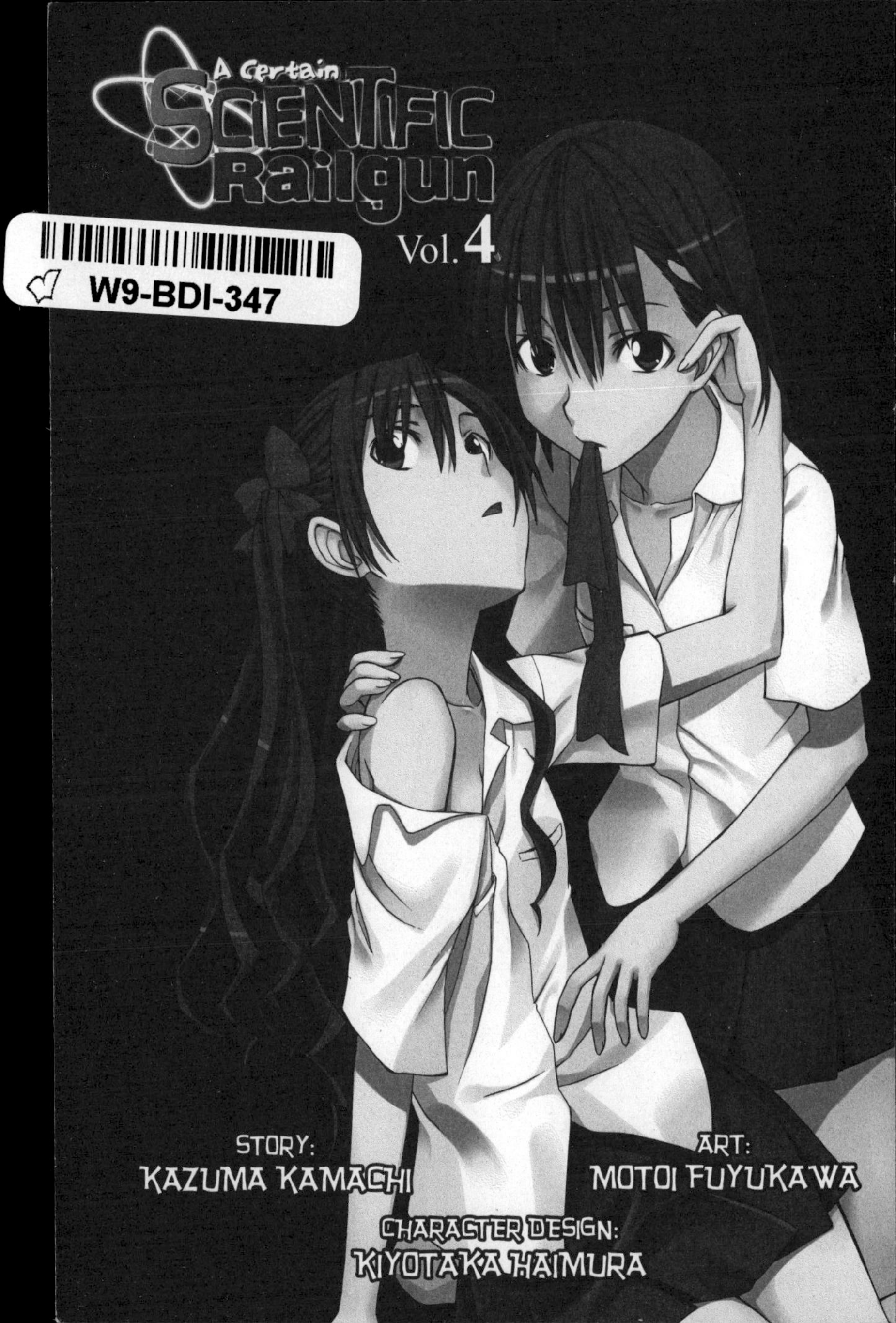
A Certain
SCIENTIFIC
Railgun
Vol. 4
STORY:
KAZUMA KAMACHI
ART:
MOTOI FUYUKAWA
CHARACTER DESIGN:
KIYOTAKA HAIMURA

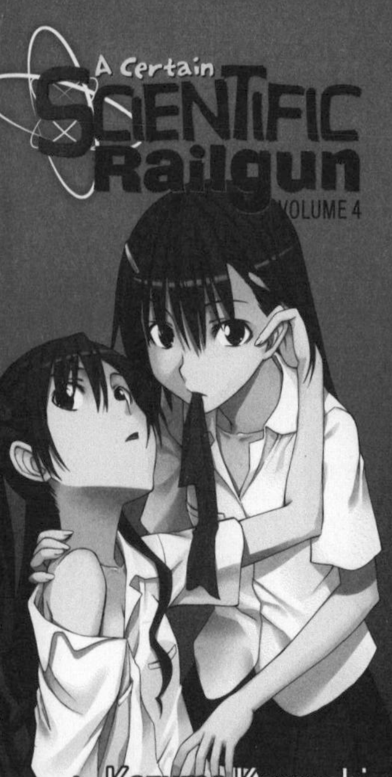

story by Kazuma Kamachi
art by Motoi Fuyukawa
Character Design Kiyotaka Haimura

STAFF CREDITS

translation	Nan Rymer
adaptation	Janet Houck
lettering	Roland Amago
layout	Bambi Eloriaga-Amago
cover design	Nicky Lim
copy editor	Shanti Whitesides
assistant editor	Maggie Danger, Alexis Roberts
editor	Jason DeAngelis
publisher	Seven Seas Entertainment

ISBN: 978-1-935934-18-9

Printed in the USA

First Printing: May 2012

10 9 8 7 6 5 4 3 2 1

READING DIRECTIONS

This book reads from *right to left*, Japanese style. If this is your first time reading manga, you start reading from the top right panel on each page and take it from there. If you get lost, just follow the numbered diagram here. It may seem backwards at first, but you'll get the hang of it! Have fun!!

CLANK
DRAG
CLANK
SHF
SHF
DID HE HURT HIS LEG?
NO. HE HAS A DISEASE CALLED MUSCULAR DYSTROPHY.
MUS-CULAR... DYS?
THUD

OH!
IT'S AN ILLNESS WHERE THE MUSCLES DETERIORATE OVER TIME.
PLOP
PLIP
PLIP
HFF
HFF
CLINK
HE WAS BORN SHOULDERING THE BURDEN OF THIS TERRIBLE DISEASE...
CLENCH
WHICH IS WHY HE'S FIGHTING IT WITH EVERY FIBER OF HIS BEING.
PULL

BUT NO MATTER HIS EFFORTS, THE DETERIORATION OF HIS MUSCLES WILL NEVER STOP.
WITH ALL OF OUR ADVANCES IN MEDICINE, WE STILL DON'T HAVE A FUNDAMENTAL TREATMENT FOR HIS DISEASE.
HE WON'T EVEN BE ABLE TO STAND UP SOON.
EVENTUALLY, HE WON'T BE ABLE TO BREATHE ON HIS OWN, AND HIS HEART WILL SUFFER A SERIES OF COMPLICA-TIONS...
BUT THAT'S ONLY HIS FUTURE IF NOTHING CHANGES.
BY USING YOUR POWER, IT MAY BE POSSIBLE TO ONE DAY SAVE THAT BOY--AND OTHERS LIKE HIM.

COMMANDS ISSUED BY THE BRAIN ARE RELAYED TO THE MUSCLES THROUGH ELECTRICAL IMPULSES.
IF WE WERE ABLE TO MANIPULATE THAT BIOELECTRICITY, THEN WE MIGHT BE ABLE TO MOVE A PERSON'S MUSCLES WITHOUT HAVING TO UTILIZE THE BODY'S NERVOUS CIRCUITRY.
BY EXPLORING YOUR ABILITIES AS AN ELECTRO-MASTER AND "PLANTING" SUCH ABILITIES INTO ANOTHER PERSON, WE MAY BE ABLE TO CONQUER MUSCULAR DYSTROPHY, ONCE AND FOR ALL.
THAT BEING SAID, WOULD YOU BE WILLING TO PROVIDE US WITH A MAP OF YOUR DNA?

SURE!
THANK YOU.

CHIRP
CHIRP
CHIRP
BLINK
NNH...
A DREAM THAT HAPPENED SO LONG AGO...?
THWACK

CHAPTER 18: AUGUST 10 (1)

WAIT UP! PLEASE...!
SHUT IT, PERVERT.
I JUST WANTED TO FEEL THE WARMTH OF ANOTHER HUMAN BEING, THAT'S ALL~!
A-ANYWAY, WHERE ARE YOU HEADED OFF TO TODAY, ONEESAMA?
HMM...
YOU KNOW HOW THEY ALWAYS HOLD THAT AREA-WIDE FIELD TRIP AT THE START OF SEPTEMBER?
THEY STILL HAVEN'T DECIDED WHERE WE'RE GOING YET.
I WAS THINKING OF PICKING UP SOME TRAVEL STUFF FOR THAT.
SIGH...
IN OTHER WORDS, YOU'RE GOING OFF ON ANOTHER ONE OF YOUR KIDDIE JUNK SHOPPING SPREES.
LIKE YOU DON'T HAVE ENOUGH WEIRD TOOTH-BRUSH AND BATH KITS ALREADY...

THEN WE'RE GOING ON A SHOPPING DATE TODAY.
I COULD GO ALONE.
WHAT ?!
ER, SO WHAT ELSE WERE YOU THINKING OF PICKING UP TODAY?
HM?
OH, NOTHING!
MAYBE SOME KIND OF DEVICE THAT DETERS PERVERTS WHO SNEAK INTO BEDS...?
ACK
SO SHE'S STILL ANGRY.
I... I WOULD BE OF GREAT ASSISTANCE TO YOU IF I CAME ALONG.
FOR EXAMPLE... IF YOU WANTED TO GO TO THE SHOPPING MALL, THEN I HAPPEN TO KNOW A SHORTCUT RIGHT OVER HERE.

WOW.
I'M SURPRISED YOU KNOW BACKALLEYS LIKE THIS.
MY HEAD IS PACKED WITH CITY MAPS, THANKS TO MY JOB.
OH...
THERE'S SOMEONE ELSE HERE.
SHIMMY
SHIMMY
SHIMMY
SQUEEZE
SQUEEZE
THIS ALLEY IS SO NARROW... IT MUST BE PRETTY ANNOYING WHEN YOU RUN ACROSS OTHER FOLKS.
W-WELL, THAT HARDLY EVER HAPP--
ANO-THER ONE?!

THIS IS SO STRANGE.
I DON'T REMEMBER EVER SEEING ANYONE COME THROUGH HERE BEFORE...
PLOP
SKRE
SKRE
SQUEEK
WHY WOULD PEOPLE BE COMING THIS WAY ALL OF A SUDDEN ...?
BOMF
SLIP

WHAM
THUD
OH. HEY, ARE YOU OKAY?!
AUU-UGH...
?!
THERE'S SOMETHING ON THE GROUND OVER HERE.
WHAT IS IT?
AN ENVELOPE.
THERE'S NO NAME OR ADDRESS ON IT...
FLIT

KUROKO, YOU SHOULDN'T BE OPENING UP SOME-THING THAT DOESN'T BELONG TO YOU.
I DIDN'T. IT WAS ALREADY OPEN.
HUH?! IS THIS...
A CASH CARD?

YOU FOUND ONE, TOO, SHIRAI-SAN?

"TOO"?
THE PAST FEW DAYS, I'VE BEEN GETTING REPORTS OF PEOPLE FINDING CASH CARDS ALL OVER THE SEVENTH SCHOOL DISTRICT.
THERE HAVE BEEN 48 CASES... NO, WAIT. IT'S JUMPED TO 56 NOW.
KLIK KLIK

*Armed Level 0 gangs in Academy City. They fight (in mobs) for the rights of those

ONEE-SAMA.
I'M TERRIBLY SORRY, BUT PERHAPS WE COULD CONTINUE OUR DATE AT A LATER TIME...?
FWOOSH
MY HEART IS BEING TORN IN DIFFERENT DIREC-TIONS!
WHY DON'T YOU START BY PATROLLING THIS AREA?
NO PROBLEM THERE. I'LL GO BY MYSELF!
I WONDER WHY ANYONE WOULD PLANT ALL THOSE CARDS.
IF THEY'VE GOT THAT MUCH MONEY TO SPARE, WHY NOT JUST DONATE IT?
HM?
SNIFF
SNIFF SNIFF

HRM... I GUESS THERE AREN'T ANY MORE LYING AROUND HERE.
HEY... SATEN-SAN?
WHAT THE HECK ARE YOU DOING?
OH! MISAKA-SAN!!
ARE YOU HUNTING FOR CARDS, TOO?
HI HI!
UM... NOT REALLY.
H-HI.
TA-DA!!
I'VE ALREADY FOUND FOUR OF THEM!
WOW, THAT'S AMAZING.
I GUESS MY NOSE WORKS REALLY WELL WHEN IT COMES TO SNIFFING OUT FREEBIES.
THAT MUST COME IN HANDY...

EH?
GRAB
TMP
TMP
OKAY! LET'S GO THIS WAY NEXT!
TMP
TMP
HEY!!
BUT I DON'T WANNA...
MY, MY. LOOK HOW DARK IT'S GOTTEN.
LET'S BRING UIHARU WITH US NEXT TIME WE GO HUNTING, 'KAY?
MY HOUSE IS THIS WAY. TAKE CARE!
I ENDED UP WASTING THE ENTIRE DAY...
HER SHARE.
IT'S TRUE, MAN!
WHAT AM I GONNA DO WITH THESE...?

I WENT DOWN THE ALLEY TO TAKE A PISS, AND I SAW THIS CHICK PLANTING ONE OF THOSE ENVELOPES.
SO I FOLLOWED HER.
SHE WENT INTO A BUILDING BIG ENOUGH FOR A FEW TENANTS...
BUT FROM WHAT I COULD TELL, IT'S JUST HER IN THERE-- SO IT'LL BE *EASY*.

'SCUSE US, LADY!
SORRY TO CRASH IN ON YA, BUT BE A GOOD GIRL AND WE'LL PLAY NICE.
OUR BOSS WON'T LET US HURT WOMEN AND KIDS.
WHAT DO YOU WANT?
......
THE CASH CARDS YOU'VE BEEN LEAVIN' AROUND TOWN.
WE'RE HERE TO TAKE 'EM OFF YOUR HANDS.
SLIP

WHOA, THERE. IT WOULD BE A REAL PAIN IF YOU TRIGGERED A SILENT ALARM OR SOMETHIN'...
SO WE'LL GO THROUGH YOUR STUFF OURSELVES.
WHAT THE--? THERE'S ONLY TWO IN HERE!
NONE IN HER UNIFORM, EITHER.
WE CAME ALL THIS WAY FOR *THAT?*
WHERE ARE THE REST?
THEY AREN'T HERE. WHICH...
equals ...
TWO IN TOTAL HERE.
YOU'RE PRETTY DAMN CALM, MISSY.
IS SHE A PSYCHIC?
WHA ?!
HEH, WHATEVER. AIN'T MANY PSYCHICS THAT COULD FACE ALL OF US.
SHE'S JUST ACTING TOUGH 'CAUSE SHE KNOWS WE WON'T HURT HER.

*Literally "Grand Champion Star Festival," a city-wide sports competition between the various schools in Academy City.

AH!
STARE
WHOA!
WH-WHAT'S WITH YOU?!
YOU'VE BEEN LOOKING PALE FOR SOME TIME. ARE YOU ALL RIGHT?
LEAVE ME THE HELL ALONE!
YOUR BREATH IS UNEVEN, AND YOU'RE DRENCHED IN A COLD SWEAT.
MUMBLE
HUH ?!
HOW'D YOU NOTICE THAT...?
Because ...
FIND ANY-THING?
NADA.
GYAAA-HAHAH!

WHAT THE *HELL* ?!
WHAT'D YOU DO TO HIM?!
HE LOOKS... DEAD.
THEN SHE *IS* A PSYCHIC?
IF SHE WAS, SHE WOULD'VE FINISHED US OFF ALREADY!
B-BUT... SHE AIN'T GOT A WEAPON ON HER. HOW'D SHE--?

I HAVE AN ACTIVATION CONDITION FOR MY ABILITY, YOU SEE.
"CRITICAL."
I CAN ONLY USE IT AFTER I'VE COME INTO **PHYSICAL CONTACT** WITH AN OPPONENT.
However ...
ONCE I'VE TOUCHED MY OPPONENT, NO MATTER WHERE HE RUNS, I CAN END HIS LIFE.
GET REAL! I'VE NEVER HEARD OF A WEIRD **ABILITY** LIKE THAT.
IT'S YOUR CHOICE TO BELIEVE ME OR NOT.
BUT KNOW THAT THERE ARE A MULTITUDE OF VARIA-TIONS IN ABILITIES--SOME OF WHICH INVOLVE A PSYCHIC RECORDING AN OPPONENT'S AIM FIELD TO CAPTURE OR INTERFERE WITH LATER.

TWITCH
THEN AGAIN, THAT CONCEPT MAY GO OVER THE HEADS OF LEVEL 0s LIKE YOURSELVES.
WHAT A STUPID BLUFF.
YOU KNOW THAT THING ABOUT US NOT HURTING WOMEN AND KIDS? THAT'S ONLY AS LONG AS WE DON'T GET HURT.
FWEET!
CRUSH HER!!
TUG
I... I GOT TOUCHED.
IT'S JUST AN ACT. MAN UP!
THEN HOW'D SHE KILL SATOSHI?!
WHAT?
IF SHE'S TELLIN' THE TRUTH, THEN I'M GONNA DIE, MAN!
IF YOU REALLY THINK SHE'S BLUFFING, THEN WHY'RE YOU USING THAT THING AGAINST AN UNARMED GIRL?!

PSH...
IT'S NEVER GOOD WHEN FRIENDS FIGHT.
Well... I'LL DO THIS, THEN.
TOUCH
?!
NOW YOU TWO SHARE THE SAME FATE.
WHA ...
MOVE.
I'LL TAKE CARE OF THIS MYSELF.

HIKOICHI, HOLD TETSU DOWN SO HE DOESN'T GET IN THE WAY.
R-RIGHT.
FLIK
!
SHE TURNED OFF THE LIGHTS?
KRASH
AH!
CALM DOWN, YOU IDIOTS. IF YOU MOVE AROUND IN A PANIC, YOU'LL END UP TAKING EACH OTHER OUT!
SHWAP
SHWAP
!
NH.
GAH.
VWHAP
DAMN.
WHAT THE HELL'S GOING ON?
MY EYES'LL GET USED TO THE DARK SOON. I JUST HAVE TO HOLD OUT UNTIL--
FLICK
UGH!

AND THEN THERE WAS ONE.
ARE YOU FRIGGIN' SERIOUS ...?
FLIK
KLIK
NOT AGAIN!
MY EYES WERE JUST GETTING USED TO THE LIGHT, THEN SHE...

I HAVE TO TAKE HER OUT!
GRIP
I'LL SHOW HER THAT PSYCHICS ARE NOTHING MORE THAN PREY TO US SKILL-OUTS!
TAP
THERE YOU ARE!
VWHP
WHAAAM
TH-THE WALL?
MY HANDS'RE--
SHHHNNN
THROB
THROB

THE PIPE! WHERE'D IT GO?!
TAP
TAP
TAP
TAP
SWING
HA HA! IF YOU'RE GONNA COME AT ME, THEN COME!
EVEN IF I GET *TOUCHED*, I'LL JUST KILL YOU BEFORE YOU USE YOUR DAMN POWER!!
WSH
HYAAAH!!
TAKE THIS!
AND THAT!
FWSH
WSH
GAH!
SLAM

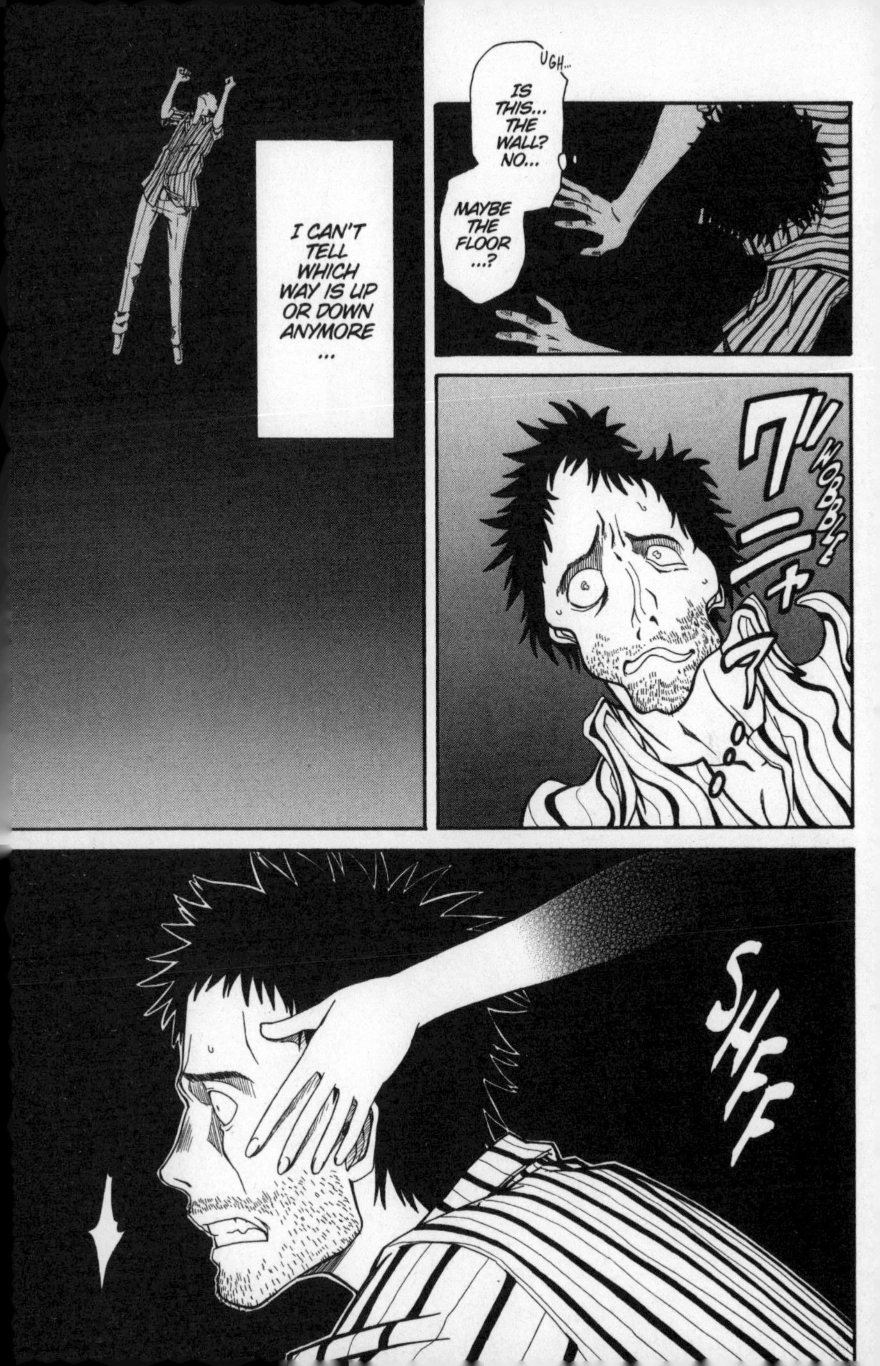
UGH...
IS THIS... THE WALL? NO...
MAYBE THE FLOOR ...?
I CAN'T TELL WHICH WAY IS UP OR DOWN ANYMORE ...
WOBBLE
SHFF

NOW YOU MEET THE CONDITION OF MY ABILITY.
DON'T WORRY. JUST LIKE YOUR FRIENDS, YOU WON'T FEEL ANY PAIN.
H-HOLD ON.
THIS WAS MY BAD. I'LL BACK OFF, I SWEAR...
AH!
FASH
ALL I NEED TO DO NOW IS LOWER MY HAND.
ST-STOP IT...!
SHVR
SHVR
VWSH!!
DON'T! PLEASE!!

PA-POP
KLIK
FLIK
FWUMP
CLAP
CLAP
CLAP
AND THE ENTIRE TIME, IT WAS NOTHING BUT A PIECE OF PAPER.

NICE. I'VE GOTTA SAY, THAT WAS REALLY ENTERTAINING.
I WAS PLANNING TO STEP IN IF THINGS GOT UGLY.
I'M CURIOUS ABOUT THE WHOLE CASH CARD THING, TOO.
USING WORDS AND A LITTLE ACTING TO BREAK THEIR SPIRITS...
YOU TOOK DOWN AN ENTIRE GROUP OF THEM. PRETTY IMPRESSIVE!
HM?
WHAT?
STARE
SO YOU'RE THE ORIGINAL.
HUH?

THE "ORIGINAL" ?
YOU'VE SURELY HEARD THE RUMORS, AT LEAST.
CHAPTER 19: AUGUST 10 (2)
RUMORS...
WAIT!
"I HEARD THEY'RE MAKING CLONES FROM THE RAILGUN'S DNA."
THEY'RE SUPPOSED TO BE USED AS MILITARY WEAPONS. THEY'RE GONNA BE RELEASED SOON."
COOL!

HMPH. THAT'S RIDICULOUS.
HUH?
YES?
DID YOU CALL MY NAME?
EH?
WHAT ?!
OH, UM...
THAT WAS DEFINITELY MISAKA-SAN.
I...
I'M SURE SHE'S MISTAKEN, BUT THIS GIRL HERE...
SHE SAYS SHE JUST SAW YOU IN THE CITY, MISAKA-SAN.
SHE WAS EVEN EMITTING ELECTRO-MAGNETIC WAVES FROM HER BODY! I CHECKED!
YOU! WHAT DO YOU KNOW ABOUT THOSE RUMORS ?!

THUNK
OW!
WHAT WAS *THAT* FOR?
YOU'RE IN MIDDLE SCHOOL, AND I'M IN HIGH SCHOOL.
THERE ARE SOCIAL CONVENTIONS WHEN ADDRESSING YOUR ELDERS.
DON'T BE SO FAMILIAR!
....
WOULD YOU HAPPEN TO KNOW ANYTHING ABOUT THOSE RUMORS, *SEMPAI*?
MORE THAN YOU DO.
ALTHOUGH IT SEEMS THAT THE PROJECT DETAILS AND OBJECTIVES HAVE CHANGED CONSIDERABLY SINCE I WAS WORKING WITH THEM.
?
THE TRUTH WOULD ONLY BRING YOU PAIN...
SINCE YOU WON'T BE ABLE TO DO ANYTHING ABOUT IT WITH YOUR POWER.
....!!

*A jumping, spinning back kick seen in Japanese pro wrestling and video games.

THE DESIRE FOR MONEY IS ESSENTIALLY FORCING PEOPLE TO NOTICE THE BACK ALLEYS, AND TO TAKE PATHS THAT THEY WOULDN'T NORMALLY TAKE.
I THOUGHT THAT IF I COULD FILL THE **GAPS** IN ACADEMY CITY'S EXTENSIVE SECURITY CAMERA SYSTEM WITH HUMAN EYES...
THEN I MIGHT BE ABLE TO STOP THE **EXPERIMENTS** THAT SUPPOSEDLY HAPPEN IN THOSE LOCATIONS.
I NEVER IMAGINED SOMEONE WOULD SEE ME HIDING THE CARDS AND FOLLOW ME BACK HERE... THAT WAS **CARELESS** OF ME.
?
?
RATTLE
HAD THEY FOUND *THIS*, THEN IT WOULD HAVE BEEN QUITE **TROUBLESOME**, TO SAY THE LEAST.
Mass Production

FLIK
LEAVING BEHIND PHYSICAL EVIDENCE IS *NEVER* GOOD.
I WAS JUST **BORROWING** THIS PLACE, ANYWAY. WE OUGHT TO LEAVE BEFORE THEY WAKE UP.
W-WAIT A MINUTE !!
PLEASE ...
GRAB
AH.
WHAT ARE YOU *TALKING* ABOUT?
WHAT EXACTLY DO YOU *KNOW* ...?

?!
Indeed, IF I'M GOING TO BE DESTROYING THE EVIDENCE, I MIGHT AS WELL DESTROY THE CRIME SCENE AND ANY WITNESSES ALONG WITH IT...
HUH ?!
THAT'S NOT--
IT'S NONE OF MY BUSI- NESS.
HOLD ON! WAIT!
WE CAN'T LEAVE THESE GUYS ...!

WEEEOOO
WEEEOOO
SNEAK
WHAT'S GOING ON? A FIRE?
SOME PUNKS WERE SLEEPING INSIDE THE BUILDING.
JUST A SMALL ONE.
MAYBE THEY DIDN'T PUT OUT THEIR CIGS.
DAMMIT! NOT ONLY DID FISH EYES SMACK ME AROUND TWICE, SHE DISAP-PEARED AFTER SPOUTING A BUNCH OF CRYPTIC CRAP!
I STILL HAVE QUES-TIONS FOR HER!

IF SHE'S FROM NAGATEN-JOUKI ACADEMY, THEN I CAN HACK INTO THEIR STUDENT DIRECTORY...
KRKL
KRKL
カシャーン
SLIDE
KLIK

ZZZKRSH
THE SECURITY RATING FOR ACADEMY CITY'S PUBLIC TELEPHONE AND INTERNET TERMINALS IS "RANK D."
THE INFORMATION TERMINALS USED BY THE SCHOOL EDUCATORS ARE "RANK B."
BUT IF I USE MY **POWERS...**
ZZKRSH
ZZKRSH
275770-B-SUCCESS-
PI-PII

09-047AJ
09-046NZ
09-045EW
09-044BE
09-057EN
09-056EH
09-055EJ
09-054VE
HMM...
09-087 IX
THERE SHE IS!!

09-087 IX
OBU NUNOTAB
NUNOTABA SHINOBU, A THIRD YEAR HIGH SCHOOL STUDENT. SEVENTEEN YEARS OLD.
SHE DISTINGUISHED HERSELF IN BIOLOGICAL PSYCHIATRY AT A TENDER AGE...
AND AFTER A RESEARCH STINT AT HIGUCHI PHARMACEUTICALS' SEVENTH MEDICAL RESEARCH CENTER...
SHE RETURNED TO NAGATENJOUKI ACADEMY.

HIGUCHI PHARMACEUTICALS, SEVENTH MEDICAL RESEARCH CENTER.
ISN'T THAT WHERE THEY'RE DOING RESEARCH ON MY DNA MAP...?
IF I GO AFTER FISH EYES AGAIN, SHE'LL PROBABLY JUST GIVE ME THE SLIP.
DON'T BE SO FAMILIAR!
FINE!
SNAP
I'LL INFILTRATE THE PLACE AND SEE FOR MYSELF!

OH...
STUMBLE
THIS UNIFORM WON'T WORK.
IF ANYONE SEES IT, THEY'LL KNOW SOME-THING'S UP.
LA MANCHA
L BANK
I'D LIKE TO USE MY CARD, PLEASE.
...OF COURSE.
PI

WELL...
A SPOILED RICH GIRL WHO GETS A HOTEL ROOM INSTEAD OF A COIN LOCKER.
I GUESS THIS'LL HAVE TO DO.
TUG
HIGUCHI PHARMACEUTICALS, SEVENTH MEDICAL RESEARCH CENTER.

Reception
YAAAWN!
TRANS-FORMATION!
MAGICAL POWERED KANAMIN!
I'LL SHOW YOU... ZSKCH
SPLENDIDLY! ZZSKRCH
ZZSKRCHZZZ
WHAT?
ZZSKKKRCHZZ
I JUST GOT THIS THING... WHAT THE HECK?
BAM BAM
WSH

OH...
GOOD, IT'S WORKING AGAIN.
WHIRRR
PII
KA-TUNK
ガゴン
WHIRRR

DAM-MIT...!
I LOST AGAIN!
THAT MEANS YOU GET TO MAKE THE ROUNDS. THANKS, MAN!
NOT AGAIN!
KREAK
BUT SERIOUSLY, IS THERE ANY POINT IN MAKING PHYSICAL PATROLS OF THIS PLACE? IT'S A SECURE FACILITY.
OFF!!
HEY, I DON'T MAKE THE RULES.
DON'T WASTE YOUR TIME COM-PLAINING. JUST DO IT.
YEAH, YEAH.

SECURITY CAMERAS, INFRARED SENSORS, AND ELECTRONIC LOCKS, HUH...?
SINCE IT'S ALL ELECTRICITY-BASED, I WON'T HAVE ANY PROBLEMS.
I SHOULD BE MORE WORRIED ABOUT THE EMPLOYEES AND SECURITY GUARDS...
KLIK
TAPPITY TAP
TAP
......?
*LAN = Local Area Network.
THAT'S WEIRD. I DON'T SEE ANY RESEARCH STATIONS MATCHING WHAT I'M LOOKING FOR.
NO... SCRATCH THAT.
THERE'S AN ISOLATED SECTION HERE THAT HAS POWER, BUT ISN'T CONNECTED TO THE LAN*.

I WONDERED WHY THE CAMERAS WERE ONLY LOCATED ALONG THE SERVICE CORRIDORS. IT LOOKS LIKE THESE RESEARCHERS DON'T WANT ANYONE...
NOT EVEN THE OTHER SECTIONS, FINDING OUT WHAT THEY'RE WORKING ON.
GUESS I'LL CHECK OUT THAT AREA FIRST.
VWHP
WHO'S THERE ?!
!!

I COULD'VE SWORN I HEARD SOMETHING...
CRAP.
IS SOMEONE-ONE THERE?!
TMP
CRAPPITY CRAP! I COULD KNOCK HIM OUT WITH MY ELEC-TRICITY...
B-THMP
B-THMP
B-THMP
BUT I REALLY DON'T WANT TO LEAVE A TRAIL.
WHAT ELSE CAN I--?

TP
TP
TP
TP
!
PI PI PI
OH, IT'S JUST THE SECURITY ROBOT.

PI PI PI
YEAH, WHAT WAS I THINKING? OF COURSE THERE WOULDN'T BE ANYONE ELSE AROUND HERE.
DID YOU SEE ANYTHING OUT OF PLACE, LITTLE GUY?
I do not report any abnor-malities.
HEH. GUESS I GET TO CUT MY PATROL SHORT THEN. THANKS.
WHEW
BWEEEP!!
BWEEEP
BWEEEEP!!

BWEEEP
THE ALARM ?!
WHAT THE HECK ?!
BWEEEP
?
?
BWEEEP
BUT WHY ?!
THE SENSORS SHOULDN'T HAVE REACTED TO ME!
DID I MESS UP SOMEHOW ?
BWEEEP
BWEEEP
I'VE GOTTA GET OUT OF HERE...
GLARE
WHIRRR

HUH ?!
SPIN
RATTLE
RATTLE
SPIN
BWEEEEP
THIS IS SO NOT MY NIGHT!
WHRL
WHRL
WHRL
WHRL
WHRL
BWEEEEP
BWEEEEP
WHAT DO I DO? TURN BACK ?!
NO. I DON'T THINK I'M THE ONE THEY'RE LOOKING FOR. THIS CONFUSION MIGHT ACTUALLY GIVE ME MY BEST SHOT.
I DON'T WANNA COME BACK HERE LATER TO FIND STRONGER SECURITY.
BWEEE

OKAY!
LET'S DO THIS!
BWEEEP
HEY! WHAT'S UP WITH ALL THESE ALARMS ?!
BWEEEP
?
CRAP, I TOTALLY FORGOT. WE WERE SUPPOSED TO HAVE A VISITOR OR SOMETHING TODAY.
BWEEEP
SAY AGAIN?! I CAN'T HEAR A DAMN THING YOU'RE SAYING!
BWEEEP
WAIT RIGHT THERE. I'M ON MY WAY TO YOU.
BWEEEP
WHO'S THERE ?!

......?
THIS IS...

IS THAT... A CULTI-VATION MACHINE?
BUT IT'S BIG ENOUGH FOR A PERSON TO FIT INSIDE...
GULP
WHO ARE YOU?
YOU OBVIOUSLY DIDN'T JUST WANDER IN HERE BY YOURSELF.

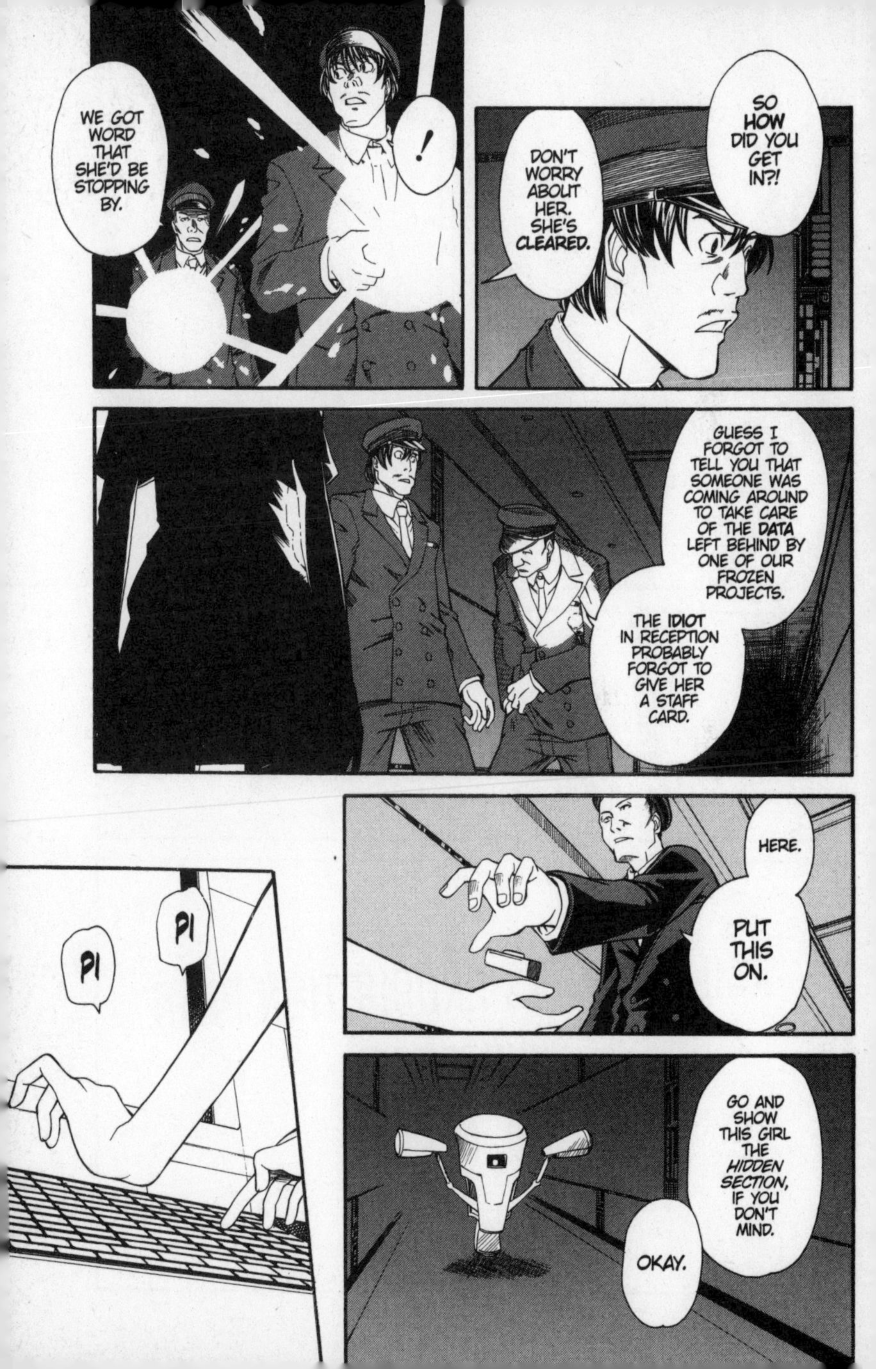
SO HOW DID YOU GET IN?!
DON'T WORRY ABOUT HER. SHE'S CLEARED.
!
WE GOT WORD THAT SHE'D BE STOPPING BY.
GUESS I FORGOT TO TELL YOU THAT SOMEONE WAS COMING AROUND TO TAKE CARE OF THE DATA LEFT BEHIND BY ONE OF OUR FROZEN PROJECTS.
THE IDIOT IN RECEPTION PROBABLY FORGOT TO GIVE HER A STAFF CARD.
HERE.
PUT THIS ON.
GO AND SHOW THIS GIRL THE *HIDDEN SECTION,* IF YOU DON'T MIND.
OKAY.
PI
PI

RAILGUN MASS PRODUCTION PLAN
"SISTERS"
FINAL REPORT

THIS PROJECT'S PURPOSE IS TO UNCOVER THE DNA PROGRAMMING PATTERNS THAT ARE REQUIRED TO PRODUCE LEVEL 5 PSYCHICS/ESPERS.
PI
PI
THIS IS TO BRING ABOUT AN INTENTIONAL 100% REPRODUCTION RATE OF LEVEL 5s, FORMALLY BORN THROUGH PURE CHANCE.
THE PROJECT'S ORIGINAL SUBJECT IS THE "RAILGUN," MISAKA MIKOTO.

*A process known as somatic-cell nuclear transfer (SCNT).

THEN THAT ...!
IN ORDER TO SHORTEN THE TIME REQUIRED TO SECURE A VIABLE TEST SAMPLE, IT WAS NECESSARY TO HASTEN THE DEVELOPMENTAL SPEED OF THE BODY AND MIND.
BASIC INTRA-CEREBRAL INFORMATION WAS PLACED UNDER THE SUPERVISION OF AN OUTSIDE STAFF MEMBER, NUNOTABA SHINOBU, WHO EMPLOYED "TESTAMENT" FOR THE INSTALLATION.
THIS WAS THEIR GOAL FROM THE VERY BEGIN-NING?!
BY ADMINISTERING Zid-02, Riz-13, AND Hel-03 TO THE SUBJECTS, WE WERE ABLE TO COMPLETE A PHYSICAL COPY OF THE RAILGUN IN APPROXIMATELY FOURTEEN (14) DAYS.
BUT MORE IMPOR-TANTLY...

BECAUSE OF THAT...
AFTER CONFIRMING THE THEORY BEHIND THE PROCESS OF MASS-PRODUCING THE "SISTERS," THE PROJECT WAS MOVED TO THE NEXT STEP. WE WERE TO BEGIN CONSTRUCTION OF THE MASS PRODUCTION SUPPORT SYSTEMS FOR THE "SISTERS."
HOWEVER...
IN THE FINAL STAGES, AN UNFORESEEN YET DEVASTATING SITUATION CAME TO LIGHT AFTER RUNNING A SIMULATED FORECAST WITH THE "TREE DIAGRAM."

Rail Gun
1,000,000,000v over
Clone
10,000,000v
THE SPECS OF THE "SISTERS" DO NOT REACH EVEN 1% OF THOSE OF THE ORIGINAL SUBJECT, THE "RAILGUN."
ON AVERAGE, A "SISTER'S" SPEC IS ON PAR WITH THAT OF A LEVEL 2. EVEN THE STRONGEST OF SUCH CLONES COULD NEVER SURPASS THE ABILITIES OF A LEVEL 3.
THEY WERE ONLY ABLE TO CREATE WEAKER VERSIONS OF ME?
IF THEY COULD ONLY CREATE LEVEL 2s, THEN IT WOULDN'T BE WORTH THE EFFORT.
DESPITE THE DNA MANIPULATION AND IMPLANTATION OF ACQUIRED KNOWLEDGE, IT WAS DEEMED IMPOSSIBLE TO CREATE A LEVEL 5 OUT OF A CLONE'S BODY.
HAVING RECEIVED THIS FORECAST, IN ORDER TO MINIMIZE ANY FURTHER EXPENSES WITH THIS PARTICULAR PROJECT...
THE COMMITTEE ORDERED US TO IMMEDIATELY HALT OUR RESEARCH.

THE RAILGUN MASS PRODUCTION PLAN, "SISTERS," WAS CANCELLED AND FROZEN INDEFINITELY.
OUR RESEARCH TEAM WAS SLOWLY DISBANDED, WHILE ANY AND ALL DATA, IN ACCORDANCE WITH ESTABLISHED PROTOCOL...
STAGGER
THUD

SO THERE WEREN'T ANY CLONES OF ME RUNNING AROUND, AFTER ALL.
SHEESH.
HA.
AHA HA HA...
I'M SURE THAT SILLY RUMOR TOOK ON A LIFE OF ITS OWN AFTER SOMEONE LEAKED A FEW DETAILS ABOUT THIS INSANE PROJECT.
YUP, THAT'S GOTTA BE IT.
KRKL
FLICKER
VWSH
BUT IT DID GIVE ME THE CHILLS FOR A SECOND THERE.
TO THINK THAT THE DNA MAP I GAVE THEM...
WHAT-EVER.
NO USE DWELLING ON THE PAST. WHAT'S DONE IS DONE.

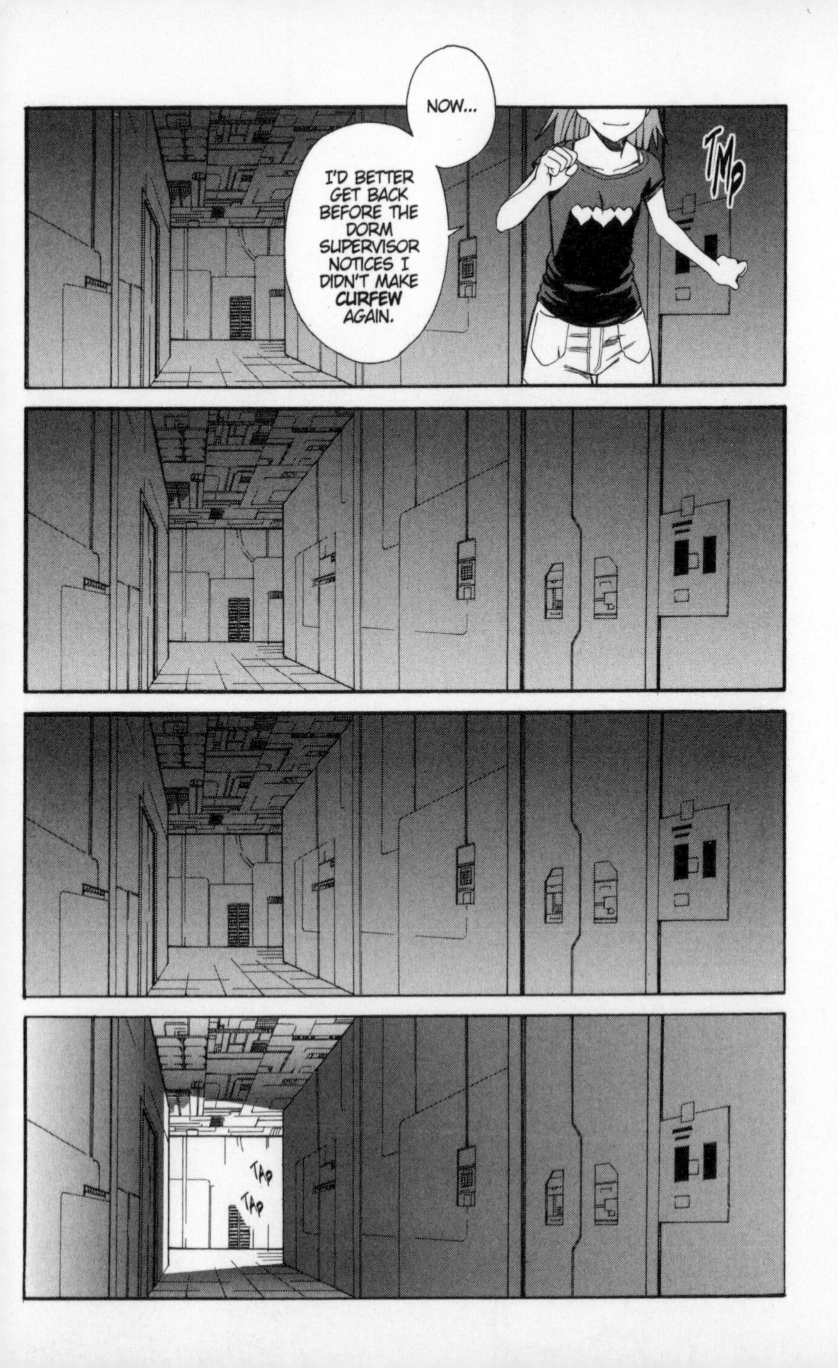
NOW...
I'D BETTER GET BACK BEFORE THE DORM SUPERVISOR NOTICES I DIDN'T MAKE CURFEW AGAIN.
TMP
TAP
TAP

WHUUUUN
VWSH
PI
PI PI PI PI
PI
delete from...
MISAKA ACCURATELY REPORTS THE FOLLOWING TIME...
42.28 SECONDS UNTIL DATA PURGE IS COMPLETED.
HEY...
HOW MUCH LONGER DO YOU THINK THIS IS GOING TO TAKE?

PI PI PI
WHRRRRR
PI PI PI PI

CHAPTER 20: AUGUST 11

♪
RUSTLE
THE SUNSHINE SPILLING THROUGH THE TREES IS SO BRIGHT TODAY.

I DON'T WANNA GET SUN-BURNED...
BUT IT WOULDN'T BE SUMMER IF IT WASN'T SO NICE AND HOT!
CHIRR
CHIRR
CHIRR
HEY, LOOK! A CICADA'S HUSK! ♡
I'VE NEVER SEEN ONEESAMA ACT SO SICKEN-INGLY SWEET.
UNTIL A FEW DAYS AGO, SHE WAS CONSTANTLY DISTRACTED. BUT NOW...
KUROKO.
AH, YES?

WHAT DO YOU WANT TO DRINK?
IT'S MY TREAT!
WAIT, THAT'S TOKIWADAI'S LEGENDARY BROKEN VENDING MACHINE! SHE NORMALLY JUST THROWS IT A ROUND-HOUSE KICK TO GET A DRINK!!
BUT SHE'S OFFERING TO BUY ONE FOR ME!
HYAAAH!
HM?
ER...
UM...
I... I'LL HAVE AN ICED COFFEE, PLEASE.
TP TP
TRIP

WHOA!
WHUMP
POFF
I-I-I'M SO SORRY! I WASN'T THINKING ANY ILLICIT THOUGHTS ABOUT WANTING TO JUMP INTO YOUR ARMS, ONEESAMA! MY FOOT WAS MERELY CAUGHT BY A PROTRUSION IN THE GROUND, AND I TRIPPED, AND--!
WSH
AHA HA HA...
I KNOW THAT. JUST BE CAREFUL FROM NOW ON, SILLY!
POKE
EH?
GOSH, ISN'T THE BREEZE JUST LOVELY ON A DAY LIKE THIS?
FLUFF
S...

SOMETHING ISN'T RIGHT.
MAYBE I'LL HAVE A COCONUT CIDER.
BUT 500ml*? I'M NOT SURE I CAN DRINK ALL THAT.
*That's nearly 17 fl oz. Your average soda can is only 12!
ON ANY OTHER DAY, I WOULD HAVE BEEN ELECTROCUTED!!
WHAT'S WITH THIS BEAUTIFUL AND KIND-HEARTED ONEESAMA?
COULD IT BE...
AN IMPOSTER?!
HM?
TAP
Y-YOUR UNDERWEAR YESTERDAY WAS A LIGHT YELLOW KIDDIE BRAND.

SIZZLE
WHY WOULD YOU SAY THAT OUT OF NOWHERE ?!
N-NO REASON.
YEAH, SHE'S DEFINITELY THE REAL ONE.
HUH?
I AM?
HONESTLY, IT WAS RATHER CREE--
ER, IT JUST SEEMED UNCHARACTERISTIC OF YOU.
WELL, I FINALLY GOT OUT OF THIS FUNK I WAS IN.
GUESS IT PUT ME IN A WEIRDLY GOOD MOOD.
SORRY, SORRY.
IF THERE'S EVER SOMETHING BOTHERING YOU, I'D BE MORE THAN HAPPY TO LISTEN...
IT JUST SEEMED TOO RIDICULOUS TO BRING UP.
FOR A SECOND THERE, I THOUGHT YOU WERE A FAKE ONEESAMA!

AH?!
NO, NO! IT HAD *NOTHING* TO DO WITH THOSE RUMORS!!
IT'S FINE. DON'T WORRY ABOUT IT.
ALL THAT CLONE STUFF SOUNDED LIKE SOME LAME SCI-FI MOVIE.
HEY, WHAT WOULD *YOU* DO IF A KUROKO CLONE SUDDENLY SHOWED UP?
AHA HA HA HA...
YEAH, THAT WOULD BE WEIRD.
BUT A CLONE MIGHT COME IN HANDY, IN CERTAIN SITUATIONS.
IF I WAS GOING TO BE LATE COMING HOME, I WOULD LEAVE HER BEHIND TO FOOL THE DORM SUPER-VISOR.
AH, THERE YOU ARE.
SALUTE
OR I'D HAVE HER DEAL WITH ANY LEC-TURES FROM SEMPAI IN MY STEAD.
GROWL
RAWR
SNAP
SNARL

AND LATER ON, WE'D REST OUR FORE-HEADS TOGETHER TO SHARE THE DAY'S MEMORIES. IT WOULD BE PERFECT!
WHAT IS SHE, YOUR ROBOT SLAVE?
WHAT ABOUT YOU, ONEESAMA? WHAT WOULD YOU DO IF *YOUR* CLONE SUDDENLY APPEARED IN FRONT OF YOU?
HMM...
GULP
I SUPPOSE ...
BURBLE
ゴポ

THREE MONTHS EARLIER.
AT A CERTAIN RESEARCH CENTER WITHIN ACADEMY CITY.
BURBLE
BURBLE
BURBLE
ALL RIGHT.
WHY DON'T I GO OVER THIS FOR FUTURE REFERENCE?
I WOULD APPRECIATE THAT.
PI
WE'VE GROWN *THIS* ONE INTO A VIABLE TEST SUBJECT.
IT STARTED AS A FERTILIZED EGG FOURTEEN DAYS AGO.

BURBLE
BURBLE
GURGLE
GURGLE
プニュ
PFHUUU
POP
STAGGER
OH, WOW...
IT LOOKS LIKE A REAL HUMAN BEING.
OF COURSE IT DOES.
SLUMP

A CLONE SHOULD LOOK LIKE THE REAL THING.
SHF
FWEE...
WAAAH——
BUT AS YOU CAN SEE, ITS CURRENT MENTAL AGE IS ON PAR WITH THAT OF A NEWBORN.
IT DOESN'T UNDERSTAND WORDS AND CAN'T WALK ON ITS OWN.

KERFLUFF
WHAT ARE YOU DOING...?
RUB RUB
I THOUGHT IT MIGHT CATCH COLD, SITTING AROUND LIKE THAT.
WE DON'T HAVE *TIME* TO DO THAT FOR EVERY DAMN ONE.
FROM WHAT I'VE HEARD, WE'RE GOING TO MAKE THEM ALL AT ONCE.
I HEARD ABOUT THAT... BUT DOESN'T THAT LOWER THEIR OVERALL EFFECTIVE-NESS?
IF WE DON'T KEEP FINE-TUNING AND ADJUSTING THEM, THEY WON'T LAST LONG.
WE SHOULD ONLY MAKE AS MANY AS WE NEED...
THE HIGHER-UPS HAVE THEIR REASONS.
ALL *WE CAN* DO IS FOLLOW ORDERS.
?

WHIIRRR
KA-CHAK
WHIRRRR
WHIRR
SPEECH, LOGIC, MOTOR ACTIVITY, AND ALL NECESSARY INFORMATION IS INPUTTED HERE THROUGH "TESTAMENT."
PSSHHH
KLANK

BLINK
HELLO!
DO YOU UNDER-STAND WHAT I'M SAYING?
THAT IS A LEAD-IN FOR COMMON CONVER-SATION.
IN OTHER WORDS, A GREETING. MISAKA UNDER-STANDS.
AND WHAT IS YOUR SERIAL NUMBER?
MISAKA IS NUMBER 9992.
GOOD. LOOKS LIKE YOU'RE SUCCESS-FULLY CONNECTED TO MISAKA-NET.
NOW PUT THIS ON FOR ME.

SHF...
......
I'M NOT SURE WHY, BUT WHEN THEY'RE SO BLATANT AND FORTHRIGHT LIKE THAT, IT MAKES ME EMBARRASSED.
SHE'S SO NAKED...
SHOULD WE PROGRAM THEM WITH A LITTLE MORE MODESTY?
ADDING UNNECESSARY EMOTIONS COULD COME BACK TO HAUNT US, IF THEY DECIDED TO REBEL.
NO "SAFETY DEVICE" IS 100% FAILSAFE, AFTER ALL.
BESIDES, WE DON'T HAVE THE TECHNOLOGY TO ADD EMOTIONS TO THESE THINGS.
SOME GIRL GENIUS NAMED NUNO-SOMETHING WAS MANAGING THE "TESTAMENT" PROGRAMMING. WE JUST HANDLE THE REST.
I SEE...

MISAKA IS SORRY TO KEEP YOU WAITING.
WHAT IS NEXT?
MISAKA AWAITS YOUR ORDERS.
restore room
SNIP
DOES THIS LOOK RIGHT...?
IT CLEARED THE HEALTH CHECK WITH FLYING COLORS.

That's a whopping $250 a tin!!

MAYBE...
MAYBE THE TASTE WAS TOO *COMPLEX* FOR A CLONE TO APPRECIATE?
MISAKA IS WONDERING IF THIS TEA WAS PROPERLY STEEPED.
HUH? WELL...
STEEPING IS A BASIC STEP REQUIRED TO EXTRACT THE FLAVOR.
THE WATER WAS NOT HOT ENOUGH, AND MISAKA CONJECTURES THAT IT WAS NOT FRESH, EITHER.
WATER BOILED IN AN ELECTRIC KETTLE DOES NOT SUIT PROPER TEA-MAKING.
AS FOR THE MILK, ONE MUST SERVE IT IN A SEPARATE MILK PITCHER, WARMED WITH HOT WATER.
THE RATIO OF TEA LEAVES SHOULD ALSO HAVE BEEN INCREASED BY A FACTOR OF 1.7.
IN OTHER WORDS, DUE TO YOUR LACK OF FORESIGHT AND CONSIDERATION, YOU HAVE KILLED THE QUALITY OF THE TEA. MISAKA DECLARES THIS AN UTTER FAILURE.
ER...
UHHH...
SIGH
MISAKA MUST SIGH DEEPLY THAT THIS IS THE FIRST TEA MISAKA HAS EVER TASTED.
I'M BEING *SNUBBED* BY SOMETHING DRINKING ITS *FIRST* CUP OF TEA?!
AH HA HA HA!

WELL, IT'S ALMOST TIME TO MOVE OUR EXPERIMENTS OUT OF THE LAB.
IF YOU'RE LUCKY, YOU MIGHT TASTE SOME *PROPER* TEA DURING YOUR OUTSIDE TRAINING.
OUTSIDE...
WHAT IS THE WORLD LIKE, OUTSIDE OF THE RESEARCH CENTER?
HOW DO I PUT IT...?
UNLIKE *THIS* PLACE, WHICH IS TEEMING WITH CHEMICAL SMELLS, THE AIR OUTSIDE IS DELICIOUS AND CLEAN.
IS THERE SOMETHING INFUSED IN THE OUTSIDE AIR THAT STIMULATES THE PALATE?!
BUT PEOPLE ARE PACKED LIKE SARDINES IN THE CITY...
HUMAN BEINGS ARE STUFFED INTO CONTAINERS?!
SIGH...
KLIK

YUCK
WE'LL ALSO BE TESTING YOUR INTER-PERSONAL SKILLS FOR WHEN YOU VENTURE OUTSIDE.
MISAKA SHALL ACQUIRE NEWFOUND KNOWLEDGE OF THE WORLD WITH A SENSE OF WONDERMENT.
!
SNAP
MISAKA IS ALREADY CONFIDENT OF HER ABILITY TO BLEND IN WITH HUMAN BEINGS FROM THE OUTSIDE WORLD. MISAKA QUESTIONS THE NECESSITY OF SUCH A TEST.
HMPH.
MISAKA IS WELL-VERSED IN A VARIETY OF TOPICS, FROM HOW TO ORDER A HAMBURGER TO TURNING DOWN AN UNSCRUPULOUS SALESMAN...
THUS MISAKA EXTOLS HER OWN VIRTUES.
I WONDER WHY ITS KNOWLEDGE IS SO BIASED.
IF IT GOES OUTSIDE, IT MAY ENCOUNTER THE ORIGINAL.

BUT I DOUBT THAT WOULD HURT THE EXPERIMENT.
?
WHAT IS THE ORIGINAL ?
THE ORIGINAL SUBJECT OF THE "SISTERS" PROJECT.
THE ONE THAT ALL OF YOU CLONES WOULD CALL "BIG SISTER," I GUESS.
....
ONEE-SAMA...

HMM.
PHYSICAL STRENGTH, STAMINA, AND CARDIO-PULMONARY FUNCTIONS ARE ALL GOOD.
NOW THAT THAT'S DONE, WE CAN *FINALLY* USE IT IN THE EXPERI-MENTS.
THIS PROCESS IS A LOT MORE INVOLVED THAN I FIRST THOUGHT.
YOU'LL BE ISSUED THE SAME TYPE OF UNIFORM THAT TOKIWADAI MIDDLE SCHOOL STUDENTS WEAR. CHANGE INTO THAT, AND THEN--
OH... ACTUALLY, BEFORE YOU CHANGE, YOU CAN TAKE CARE OF *THIS.*
WE NEED TO GRAB FIVE OR SIX MORE CLONES ANYWAY.

THINK YOU CAN CLEAN ALL THAT UP BEFORE THE NEXT EXPERI-MENT?

IF YOU CHANGE BEFORE YOU CLEAN, YOU'LL GET YOUR UNIFORM DIRTY.
UNDER-STOOD.

CHAPTER 21: AUGUST 15 (1)

CRUNCH THAT CRISPY SEAWEED!
TASTY FRESHLY MADE
ONIGIRI!
SHWAAA
PHEW.
I WAS REALLY LOOKING FORWARD TO READING THE LATEST ISSUE...
BUT IT WAS SO *SHORT.* AND AFTER LAST WEEK WAS A DOUBLE ISSUE!

added on to their deadline while everyone else is off on holiday, making their schedule more lax. This is an inside joke by the manga-ka.

ACK!
YOU KIDS ARE FROM...
WHEN I WAS LOOKING FOR THAT BAG.
※ BACK IN VOLUME 1, CHAPTER 2!
COME PLAY WITH US!
I... I CAN'T. I'M REALLY BUSY.
LIAR! YOU JUST SAID YOU WERE FREE!
UH...
THEY HEARD THAT PART, HUH?

SIGH.
OH, ALL RIGHT. I GUESS I DON'T HAVE A CHOICE.
ONEESAN CAN PLAY.
YAAAY!!
PFFT.
ONEESAN? YEAH, RIGHT.
SHE'S NOT MUCH OLDER'N US.
THAT'S TOTALLY STUCK UP. SHE'S JUST TRYIN' TO ACT OLD.
OH YEAH?
ダ TP
ダ TP
ダ TP
まなこ
練乳
ダ TP
ダ TP
ダ TP

HYAAAH!!
COME ON, GUYS! LET'S GO!
CRAP! SHE GOT ME AGAIN!
THAT'S TEN TIMES IN A ROW...
YAY!
TAKE IT EASY, WILL YA? WE'RE ONLY IN ELEMENTARY SCHOOL!
HOW FAR DID YOU KICK THAT?!
UH...
I THOUGHT I WAS JUST ONE OF THE KIDS.

OGRE! DEMON! BEAST!!
WHAT-EVER.
SHORTY PANTS WUSS !!!
WHAT DID YOU CALL ME, YOU SNOT-NOSED BRAT?!
Tp Tp Tp Tp Tp Tp Tp
WHEN DID KICK THE CAN TURN INTO TAG?
LET ME AT THAT SMART LITTLE MOUTH!
SDOP ID, AHHN!
SONG SONG!
I-I'LL COME BACK AS A LEVEL 5 ONE DAY AND STOMP YOU!
ANY TIME, SQUIRT.
I HEARD YOU WERE A REALLY COOL ELECTRO-MASTER, ONEECHAN.

THEN YOU'RE THE SAME AS NAO-KUN.
OH, YEAH?
Y-YEAH.
BUT...
WHK
MPH ~!
CLENCH
NMPH ~!
SHK SHK SHK SHK
NPH ...!!
SPARK
I TRY AND TRY, BUT THE BEST I CAN DO IS A TINY LITTLE SPARK.
PHEW...
EVERY-ONE'S LIKE THAT IN THE BEGIN-NING.

WHEN NAO-KUN GETS BETTER, DO YOU THINK HE CAN CALL YOU?
CALL ME?
OH.
YOU KNOW, LIKE TALKING WITH ELECTRICITY.
TESTING TESTING.
I DOUBT IT. I PROBABLY COULDN'T EVEN FIND HIS *LOCATION* THAT WAY.
IF THERE WAS ABSOLUTELY NOTHING BETWEEN US, ***MAYBE*** *I COULD FEEL HIS POWER.*
OH, I FELT A LITTLE SHOCK THERE.
KRKL
BUT IN THE MIDDLE OF THE CITY, WITH ELECTRO-MAGNETIC WAVES EVERY-WHERE, THERE'S NOT MUCH CHANCE OF THAT.
KRKL
?

THEN AGAIN, THERE WAS THAT WHOLE "LEVEL UPPER" INCIDENT...
ALL THIS RUNNING MADE ME HOT AND ICKY!
OH. BOO.
I GUESS PEOPLE WITH SIMILAR BRAINWAVE PATTERNS COULD FORM A SORT OF NETWORK WITH EACH OTHER.
NOT VERY LIKELY, THOUGH.
SKY

*A gachapon, a toy-dispensing machine named after the sound it makes.

UH-OH. IT'S THE KIND WHERE YOU TURN THE HANDLE AND A CAPSULE DROPS DOWN.
BRING IT!
WITH SOMETHING THIS MANUAL, MY POWERS WON'T AFFECT IT.
¥200
KA-KLUNK
¥200
KA-KLUNK
KA-KLUNK
KA-KLUNK
KA-KLUNK
KA-KLUNK
KA-KLUNK
KA-KLUNK
HEY, LOOK. SOME TOKIWADAI GIRL IS PLAYING WITH THE GACHA GACHA MACHINE.

SHE'S PROBABLY BUYING TOYS FOR ALL THOSE KIDS.
AWW. THAT'S SO NICE OF HER!
I CAN'T WIN.
THERE ARE TOO MANY KINDS!
SORRY. WOULD YOU GET SOME CHANGE FOR ME?
HUH? WHY ME...?
SONG SONG
KA-KLUNK
KA-KLUNK
DON'T ASK. LOOK AT THOSE EYES.
UH. GOOD CALL.
KA-KLUNK KA-KLUNK KA-KLUNK KA-KLUNK KA-KLUNK KA-KLUNK KA-KLUNK KA-KLUNK KA-KLUNK KA-KLUNK KA-KLUNK KA-KLUNK
EMPTY
THERE WASN'T A SINGLE ONE, HUH?

UM...
IF YOU WANT, I'LL TRADE YOU MINE...
THERE'S ANOTHER ONE IN FRONT OF THE TRAIN STATION.
ecorde+

YAY! YOU GOT ONE!
THANKS. ♡
CLAP CLAP
YEAH. THAT'S JUST GREAT.
CLAP CLAP CLAP
WITH THIS, I CAN FINALLY...

WAIT, WHAT THE HECK DO YOU USE THESE THINGS FOR?
HAVEN'T YOU EVER HAD YOUR COLLECTOR'S SPIRIT IGNITED, DRIVING YOU TO GATHER EVERYTHING THAT'S EVER BEEN MADE OF YOUR FAVORITE BRAND?
AND THEN YOU WENT AND DID IT, WITHOUT THINKING ABOUT THE CONSE-QUENCES?
EVEN I KNOW I CAN'T WEAR SOME-THING LIKE THIS ON MY SHIRT.
WORSE, I CAN ALREADY FEEL KUROKO'S EYES DRILLING INTO ME.
SIGH
AGAIN? REALLY?
WAIT... IT MIGHT BE OKAY TO PUT IT ON MY BAG...
OH, IT'S TIME TO GO HOME.
IT'S STILL SO BRIGHT OUTSIDE.
WELL, THE SUN GOES DOWN A LOT LATER IN THE SUMMER.

WHEN I WAS YOUR AGE...
KIIIIIINNN
SOME-THING WRONG, ONEE-CHAN?
?
HUH? UH...
N-NOTHING.

YOU GUYS BE CAREFUL GOING HOME, OKAY?
OKAY!
BYE BYE!
TURN
WHAT THE HECK DID I JUST FEEL...?

IT WAS A POWER LIKE MINE. NO...
IT WAS LIKE FEELING MY OWN POWER EMITTING AND WASHING BACK OVER ME--FROM THE OUTSIDE.
....
TP
IT CAN'T BE.
BUT...
BUT...!
HFF
HFF
I COULD'VE SWORN...
IT WAS COMING... FROM AROUND HERE...

!
WHA
...
WHO THE HELL ARE YOU?!

A Certain
SCIENTIFIC
Railgun

WHO THE HELL ARE YOU?!

MIAAAO...
HUH?

CHAPTER 22: AUGUST 15 (2)

MIAO?!
WHAT DOES THAT MEAN ...?
IS THAT HER NAME? IS IT THE ORGANIZATION SHE WORKS FOR? OR DID I JUST HEAR HER WRONG?
WAIT, MAYBE IT'S NOT EVEN JAPA-NESE...?
THE FOUR-LEGGED, LIVING CREATURE SAID THAT, IMPLYING DISTRESS.
MEOW.

A CAT?!
WHEN MISAKA PASSED DOWN THIS ROAD EARLIER...
MISAKA NOTICED AN INFANT LEFT INSIDE A PARKED VEHICLE.
OH NO! THIS IS BAD!!
THE ANTI-SKILL MEMBER THERE ADVISED THAT THE INFANT WAS AT RISK FOR HEAT-STROKE...
SO, MISAKA USED HER POWERS TO RELEASE THE LOCK ON THE VEHICLE'S DOOR.
THE LIVING CREATURE WAS SURPRISED BY MISAKA'S ACTIONS AND RAN UP THE TREE.
FWSH
THANKS A MIL!

NOW IT IS UNABLE TO CLIMB DOWN.
MISAKA HAS CAREFULLY RECOUNTED THE CHRONOLOGY OF EVENTS.
I SEE...
AH!
YOU DIDN'T ANSWER MY QUESTION! WHO THE HECK *ARE YOU?!*
TWITCH
OH.
IT SEEMS THAT THE CREATURE IS NOW IN A MORE PRECARIOUS PREDICAMENT.

ARE YOU SURE WE SHOULD NOT RESCUE IT?
IT'S SMALL, BUT IT'S STILL A CAT! IT'LL BE FINE IF IT DROPS DOWN FROM THERE! MORE IMPORTANTLY--
MISAKA UNDERSTANDS.
WHAT YOU'RE SAYING, ONEESAMA, IS THAT YOU WOULD NOT CARE IF THE CREATURE DASHED ITSELF AGAINST THE GROUND.
IT WOULD NOT HAVE ANYTHING TO DO WITH YOU, EVEN IF IT SUSTAINED SERIOUS INJURIES THAT LED TO THE TERMINATION OF ITS VITAL ACTIVITIES.
STARE
UGH.
FINE... WHAT DO YOU SUGGEST WE DO?
IF WE ADOPT THE FOLLOWING POSITION, WE SHOULD BE ABLE TO REACH THE CREATURE.
MISAKA PROPOSES THIS.
I DON'T SEE ANYTHING AROUND HERE WE COULD STAND ON...

WHY AM I ON THE BOTTOM ?
MORE TO THE LEFT, ONEE-SAMA.
DON'T BE RIDICU-LOUS!
YOU'RE STANDING ON ME WITH YOUR SHOES STILL ON!
WIGGLE
WIGGLE
HGHHH!
LEAP

STMP
WH-WHY YOU--!
MISAKA WAS ABLE TO SAFELY SECURE--
WAAAAAAAHHH?!!
HE... HE...
HEEEEEEY!!
WHY DID YOU FLIP YOUR SKIRT UP?!
YOU'RE AN INNOCENT MAIDEN! AN INNOCENT MAIDEN!!

YOU CAN'T DO THINGS LIKE THAT WHILE WEARING MY FACE...
MEOOOOW.
SQUEE.
SHUCKS... UP CLOSE, THIS KITTEN IS *CUTE.*
KITTEN?
WELL, IT'S A BABY CAT, SO THAT MAKES IT A KITTEN.
THEY'RE ALWAYS SO AFRAID OF ME...
?
REACH
THEY CAN'T HELP BUT REACT TO THE FAINT ELECTRO-MAGNETIC WAVES EMITTING FROM MY BODY.
TRMBL
TRMBL

SIGH.
IT SEEMS LIKE MISAKA IS ALSO DISLIKED.
ARGH!
YOU STILL HAVEN'T ANSWERED ME!!!
TWITCH
OH...
HOW DARE SHE LOWER MY GUARD WITH AN ADORABLE CAT!
SO. YOU.
ARE YOU...
MY CLONE OR SOME-THING?
YES.

NOW SHE'S UP-FRONT...
BUT I THOUGHT THAT PROJECT WAS FROZEN.
WHY ON EARTH ARE THINGS LIKE YOU WALKING AROUND?
ZXC741ASD 852QWE963' ......
MISAKA REQUESTS A CONFIRMATION PASSCODE.
HUH?
AS EXPECTED, ONEESAMA IS NOT AFFILIATED WITH THE EXPERIMENTS.
MISAKA CANNOT ANSWER YOUR QUERY, THEN.
WHO'S THE MASTERMIND BEHIND THIS PROJECT?
THAT IS CLASSIFIED.
WHY WERE YOU CREATED?
THAT IS RESTRICTED.
YANK

DO YOU WANT TO GET HURT? I COULD FORCE YOU TO TELL ME.

UGH.
FINE. JUST GO ALREADY.
I'LL BE RIGHT BEHIND YOU.
YOU'LL HEAD BACK TO SOME FACILITY OR RESEARCH CENTER EVENTUALLY.
AND WHEN I ARRIVE, I'LL GRAB YOUR CREATOR AND GET MY ANSWERS!

"SISTERS" ...
I WOULDN'T HAVE BELIEVED IT IF I HADN'T SEEN ONE RIGHT IN FRONT OF ME.
EVEN THOUGH I'D TOTALLY REJECTED IT AS A STUPID RUMOR...
I WAS ALWAYS AFRAID THAT A LOOK-ALIKE CLONE WOULD SHOW UP ONE DAY.
BUT...
TO THINK THIS THING IS AN ACTUAL CLONE...
IT'S NOT HOW I IMAGINED IT. I THOUGHT IT WOULD BE TRYING TO KILL ME AND TAKE MY IDENTITY OR SOMETHING.
I GUESS I SHOULD BE MORE SHOCKED ABOUT THIS... BUT SHE'S SO WEIRD THAT I DON'T KNOW WHAT TO THINK.
HM?
"SIS-TERS" ...?

W-WAIT A SECOND!
DON'T TELL ME THERE ARE FIVE OR TEN MORE THINGS LIKE YOU OUT THERE?
KITTEN... KONEKO (コネコ)... IT'S THE SAME IF YOU READ IT RIGHT-TO-LEFT OR LEFT-TO-RIGHT, HEE.
ARE YOU EVEN LISTENING TO ME?!
AND STOP SAYING STUPID CRAP LIKE THAT OUT LOUD!
FWAAAH.
WHAT'S THAT?
RWAR! RWAR!

HEY, YOU TWO...
SISTERS SHOULDN'T FIGHT.
SHE'S *NOT* MY SISTER!!
NOW, NOW. YOU SHOULD *NEVER* SAY STUFF LIKE THAT, EVEN AS A JOKE.
HOLD ON A SEC.
?
HERE.
TWO OF OUR BEST SELLERS!
THINK THIS WILL HELP YOU MAKE UP?
ICE CREAM?
YOU TRYING TO FORCE US TO BUY THESE?
WHAT KIND OF CREEP DO YOU TAKE ME FOR?

I WAS ABOUT TO WASH OUT THE CASES, ANYWAY.
SO THEY'RE YOURS-- NO CHARGE.
I DON'T KNOW WHAT HAPPENED BETWEEN YOU TWO...
BUT THEY SAY EATING SWEETS SOOTHES THE SOUL.
PAT
LOOK, I APPRECIATE IT, BUT THIS ISN'T THE BEST TIME FOR ICE CR--
HMM. DENSE BUT NOT HEAVY, WITH A REFRESHINGLY SWEET AFTERTASTE... IT IS OBVIOUS THAT HIGH QUALITY MILK WAS USED. HOWEVER, THIS TEXTURE WOULD NOT HAVE BEEN POSSIBLE WITHOUT A FINE GRADE OF JAPANESE SUGAR AS WELL. AS FOR THE CONE, IT IS REMINISCENT OF THE CRISPY OUTSIDE CRUST OF A FRESHLY BAKED COOKIE.
CHOMP CHOMP
GOOD JOB!
MISAKA REWARDS YOU UNHESITATING PRAISE.
AHA HA...
THANKS.

WHEN PEOPLE DIVORCE, THEY CAN BECOME STRANGERS TO ONE ANOTHER...
BUT THE BOND BETWEEN SISTERS WON'T *EVER* FADE.
SPEAKING OF DIVORCE, MY WIFE MIGHT WANT ONE IF I DON'T GO AND MAKE US SOME MONEY.
DON'T LOOK AT ME!
ANYWAY, YOU TWINS BE GOOD TO EACH OTHER!
VROOOM
I KEEP TRYING TO TELL YOU!
IT'S NOT LIKE THAT!!
WHATEVER... I GUESS THAT'S A NORMAL ASSUMPTION FOR A STRANGER TO MAKE.
WHO WOULD THINK WE SHARE THE SAME DNA *WITHOUT* SHARING BLOOD?
LICK
HUH?
WHERE'D IT GO?

HEY!
DON'T BE SO GREEDY!
WHAT ARE YOU TALKING ABOUT?
MISAKA FEIGNS IGNORANCE AS SHE CONTINUES TO SAVOR THE FRESH AFTERTASTE OF THE MINT CHOCOLATE ICE CREAM.
MISAKA'S BODY HAS BEGUN TO FEEL CHILLY, SO MISAKA WOULD LIKE TO DRINK SOME TEA NOW.
MISAKA PLEADS NONCHALANTLY...
GIVE ME A FRIGGIN' BREAK!
WHY AM I DOING THIS...?
THIS IS QUITE GOOD!
HEY, LOOK. TWINS WEARING THE TOKIWADAI UNIFORM.
IT'S NOT WHAT YOU THINK.
ONEE-SAMA, MISAKA WOULD LIKE NEXT--
ENOUGH IS ENOUGH!
WOW! THOSE TWINS--
EVERYBODY SHUT UP!
F-FLIK
SO...

WHEN EXACTLY ARE YOU PLANNING TO GO BACK HOME...?
MISAKA FORGOT TO TELL YOU, ONEESAMA.
MISAKA IS HEADING TO AN EXPERI- MENT NOW.
MISAKA WILL NOT BE RETURNING TO THE FACILITY.
WHA ?!
IT IS YOUR CHOICE TO FOLLOW MISAKA OR NOT...
BUT YOU WOULD NOT MEET MISAKA'S CREATOR THIS WAY.
WHY ARE YOU ONLY TELLING ME NOW?
BECAUSE YOU DID NOT ASK.
INDIFFERENT
.........!!

WHAT SHOULD I DO?
WOULD IT BE FASTER FOR ME TO JUST DECRYPT THAT PASSCODE SHE GAVE ME AND UNCOVER THE INFORMATION ON MY OWN?
AH, GOOD... I HAVE MY PDA WITH ME.
KLINK
WHOOPS. I FORGOT I STILL HAD THIS IN MY POCKET.
?
WHAT IS THAT?
JUST SOME PRIZE I WON OUT OF A GACHA GACHA MACHINE...

WHAT ARE YOU DOING?
JUST HOLD STILL.
KLIK
KLIK
SNAP
......
HMM... YEAH, THIS IS *WAY* BETTER THAN A MIRROR. I CAN BE A LOT MORE OBJECTIVE.
AND I THINK THAT MIGHT WORK.
NO. IT IS TER-RIBLE.
MISAKA IS ASTOUNDED BY ONEESAMA'S KIDDIE SENSE OF STYLE.
AH!
H-HOW DARE YOU!!

I-I WAS JUST KIDDING...
MY OWN CLONE TRASHING MY FASHION SENSE...
I ONLY PUT IT ON TO SEE, THAT'S ALL.
REACH
SLAP
ZING ZING
......
SLAP
PARRY
PARRY
PARRY
BLOCK
BLOCK
BLOCK

WHAT THE HECK ARE YOU DOING?!
THAT HURTS!!
OWNERSHIP OF SAID BADGE TRANSFERRED TO MISAKA WHEN ONEESAMA PLACED IT UPON MISAKA'S BODY. MISAKA INSISTS.
ONEESAMA'S CURRENT ACTIONS WOULD CONSTITUTE ROBBERY.
WHAT SORT OF TWISTED *LOGIC* IS THAT?!
IT IS NOT TWISTED.
IN ADDITION...
THIS IS THE FIRST GIFT MISAKA HAS RECEIVED FROM ONEESAMA.

DIDN'T ONEESAMA HAVE ANYTHING BETTER THAN THIS TRASH?
MISAKA HIDES MISAKA'S TRUE FEELINGS WHILE RELEASING A DEEP SIGH.
GIVE IT BACK! NOW!!
ACK, I GOT SUCKERED IN WITHOUT REALIZING IT AGAIN.
BUT I'M NOT GONNA MAKE ANY PROGRESS JUST STANDING AROUND HERE. I GUESS I SHOULD CHECK OUT WHAT I CAN FIND ONLINE FIRST...
I GIVE UP. I'M TAKING OFF FOR TODAY.
HM ...?
DID YOU WANT TO SAY SOME-THING?
NO...
GOOD-BYE.
ONEE-SAMA.
RIGHT.
SEE YA.

WHAT THE HECK WAS THAT ALL ABOUT?
THIS IS SO CONFUSING...
WE PLAYED WITH A CAT.
WE ATE ICE CREAM TOGE-THER.
THEN WE FOUGHT OVER A STUPID TIN BADGE.
IT WAS ALMOST AS IF WE WERE REALLY--
AH!
SHAKE
SHAKE

I NEED TO FOCUS ON FINDING HER CREATOR AND GETTING SOME ANSWERS!
I'LL FIGURE OUT THE REST LATER.
STATION
PI
PI
PI
KLIK

KLUNK
KREAK
バタン
I'VE BEEN SPENDING ALL MY FREE TIME WORKING ON JUDGMENT'S SUMMER RECRUIT-MENT...
MY SUMMER HOMEWORK'S NOT EVEN CLOSE TO BEING DONE!
HMM...
UH-OH.
THIS ISN'T GOOD!

A CALL FROM MISAKA-SAN?!
THAT'S ODD.
YES, HELLO?
UIHARU-SAN?
I'M SORRY TO BOTHER YOU SO LATE AT NIGHT.
OH, AND SORRY FOR BEING SO ABRUPT, BUT DO YOU HAVE ANY IDEA WHAT "ZXC741ASD85 2QWE963" MEANS?
HUH?

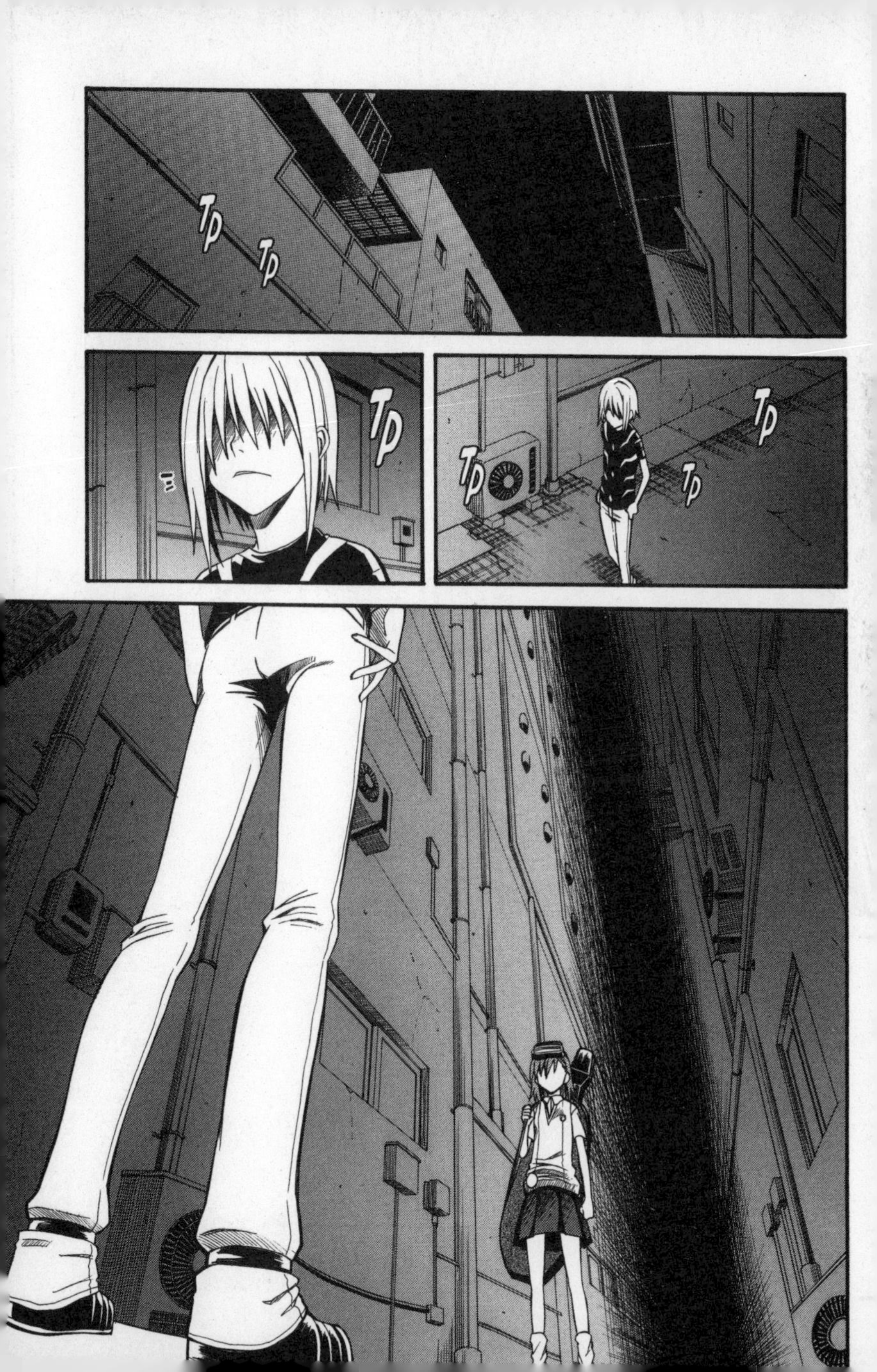
Tp
Tp
Tp
Tp
Tp
Tp

THE CURRENT TIME IS 2018 HOURS.
AS THERE ARE 11 MINUTES AND 40 SECONDS REMAINING UNTIL THE COMMENCEMENT OF THE 9982ND EXPERIMENT ...
MISAKA REQUESTS THAT WE MOVE TO THE DESIGNATED RENDEZVOUS POINT.

CHAPTER 23: AUGUST 15 (3)

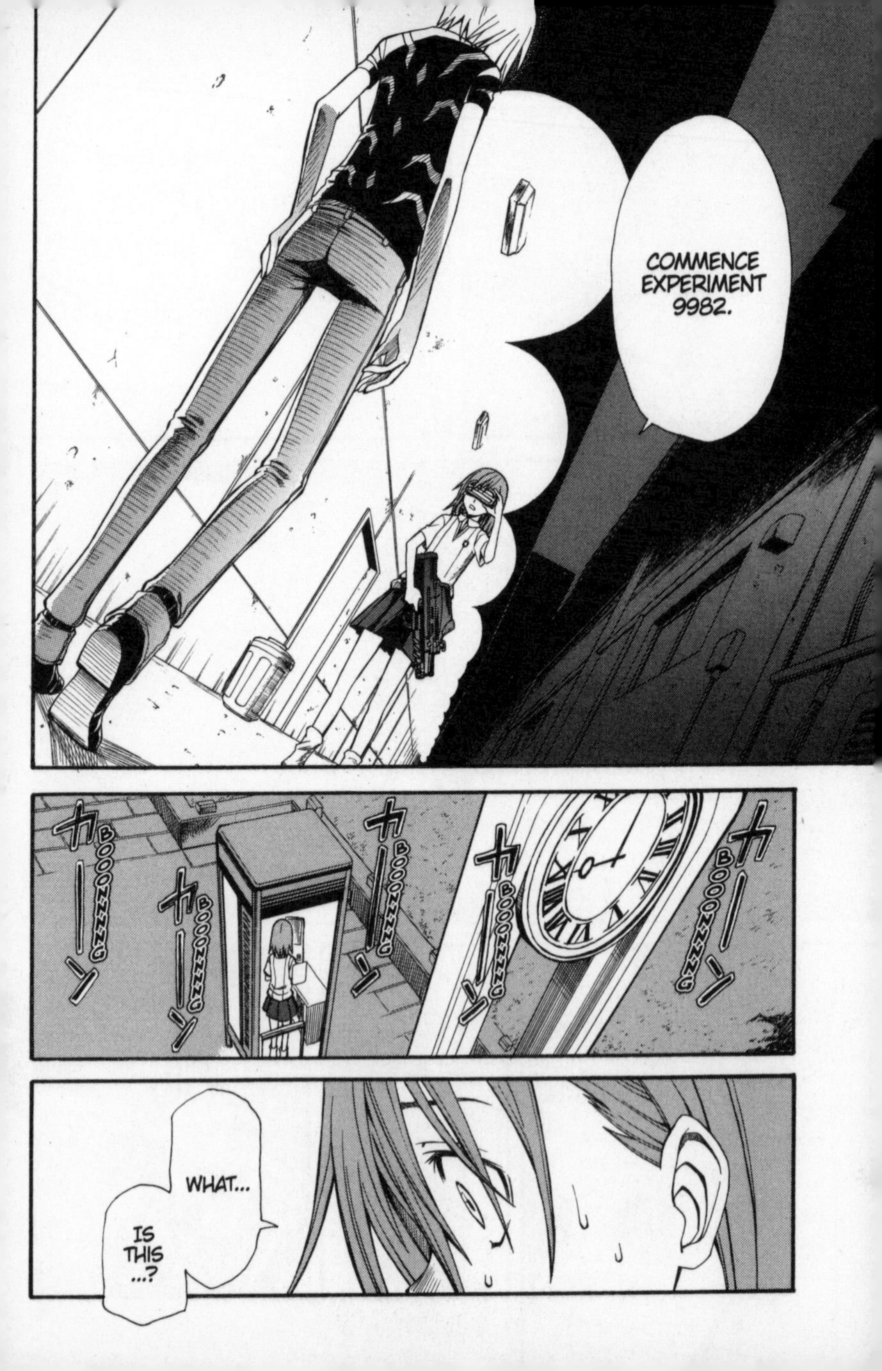
COMMENCE EXPERIMENT 9982.
カーン
BOOONNNNG
カーン
BOOONNNNG
カーン
BOOONNNNG
カーン
BOOONNNNG
カーン
BOOONNNNG
WHAT...
IS THIS ...?

A Certain
SCIENTIFIC
Railgun
CHAPTER 23: AUGUST 15 (3)

"A METHOD OF EVOLVING A LEVEL 5 INTO A LEVEL 6, THROUGH PRACTICAL APPLICATION OF THE 'SISTERS.'"
THERE ARE SEVEN LEVEL 5s WITHIN ACADEMY CITY.
ACCORDING TO SIMULATIONS RUN BY THE "TREE DIAGRAM," ONLY ONE OF THEM WAS DETERMINED TO HAVE THE POTENTIAL...
TO REACH THE YET-TO-BE-SEEN LEVEL 6.
TMP
TMP
TMP
TMP

BANG
BOOM
THUD
KLUNK
?
KRASH
NH --!
KRUNK

IF THE SUBJECT UNDERWENT MERELY THE REGULAR "CURRICULUM," IT WOULD TAKE AN ESTIMATED 250 YEARS TO REACH LEVEL 6 STATUS.
FIZZLE
KRKL

WE HAVE THEREFORE CHOSEN TO PURSUE ANOTHER METHOD, UTILIZING LIVE COMBAT TO PROMOTE GROWTH OF THE SUBJECT'S ABILITIES.
FLIK
"BY PREPARING SPECIFIC BATTLE-GROUNDS AND STAGING SET COMBAT SCENARIOS, WE CAN MANIPULATE THE SUBJECT'S GROWTH."
"WITH THIS REVISED PLAN, CALCULATED SIMULATIONS BY THE 'TREE DIAGRAM' RECOM-MENDED THAT BY PREPARING 128 DIFFERENT TYPES OF BATTLE-GROUNDS..."
"AND THEN KILLING THE 'RAILGUN' 128 TIMES ON THESE BATTLE-GROUNDS, THE TEST SUBJECT WOULD BE ABLE TO ADVANCE TO LEVEL 6."

HOWEVER, AS IT IS IMPOSSIBLE TO PROCURE MULTIPLE "RAILGUNS"...
WE ESTABLISHED AN ALTERNATIVE METHOD THROUGH THE "SISTERS" FROM THE PREVIOUSLY FROZEN "RADIO NOISE PROJECT."

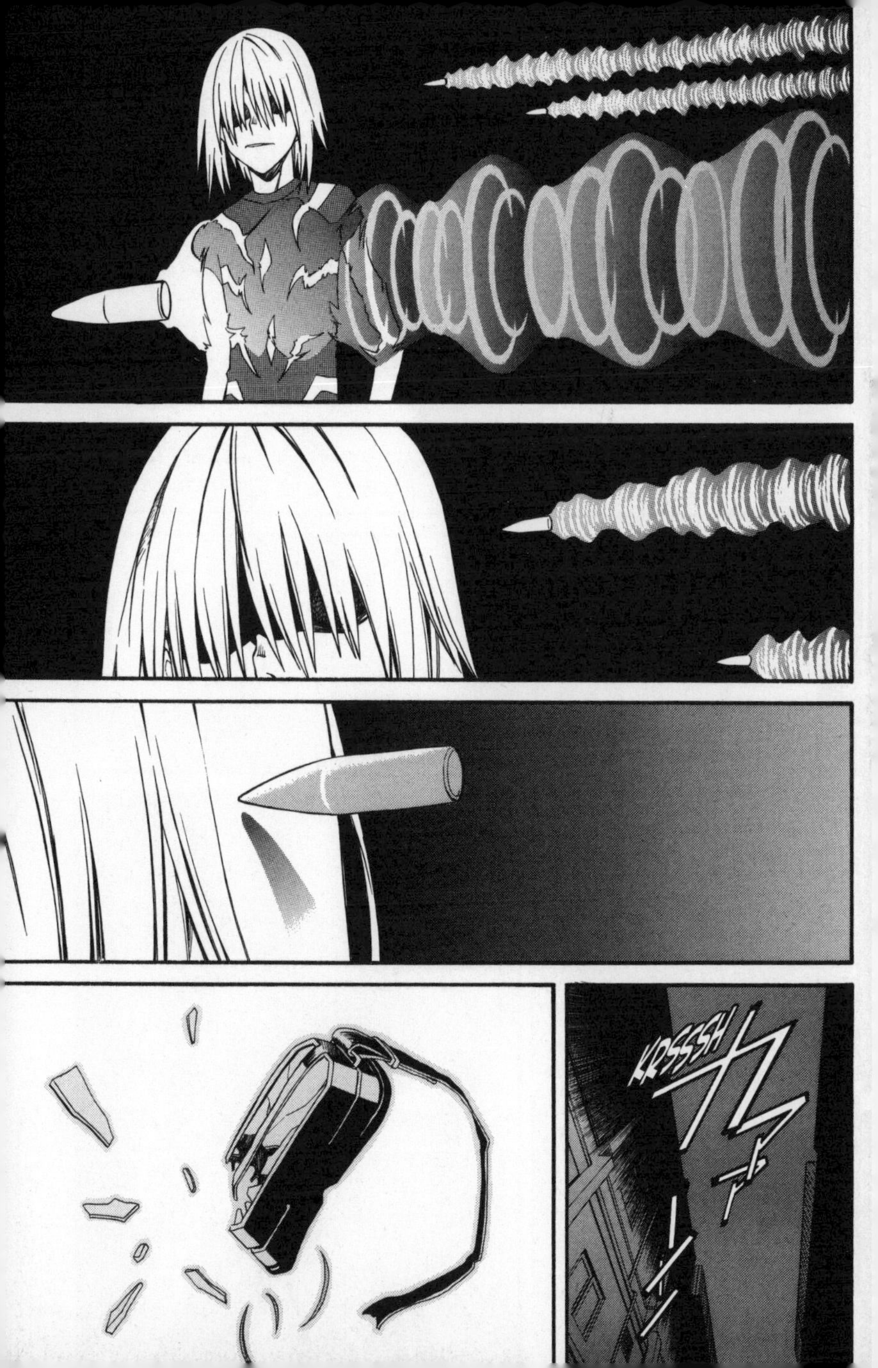
KRSSSSH

WHAM
SLIDE...
WOBBLE
......?
SHLIK
KLATTER
TMP

BY UTILIZING A LARGE NUMBER OF HEAVILY ARMED "SISTERS" AGAINST THE SUBJECT, WE CAN OVERCOME THE DEFICIENCY LEFT BY THEIR LOWER SPECS.
TP
WE CAN ACHIEVE A SHIFT TOWARDS LEVEL 6 THROUGH COMBAT WITH 20,000 "SISTERS."
AHA HA... WHAT THE HECK IS THIS?
KILLING ME, THEN KILLING MY CLONES INSTEAD OF ME, THEN ALL THIS LEVEL 6 STUFF...
IT'S TOO CRAZY TO BE A JOKE.
EXPERIMENT 9982
START TIME: AUGUST 15, 21:00
ABSOLUTE COORDINATES: X-162258 Y-415687
THERE'S NO WAY THIS CAN BE REAL...

GOODBYE.
ONEE-SAMA.
ABSOLUTE COORDINATES X-162258 Y-415687
BYE...
DAM-MIT!
KLANG
KLANG
KLANG

KLANG
KLANG
KLANG
IN THIS GAME, YOU'RE PLAYING FOR YOUR LIFE.
HA HA. RUN, RUN, AS FAST AS YOU CAN. THE LONGER YOU RUN, THE LONGER YOU'LL LIVE!
FWWHH

SWF
KWHAM

AND WHEN YOU GET CAUGHT, IT'S GAME OVER.
WSH
K-KRASH
STOMP
TOO SLOW !!

AH!
WHUNK
GAH!
!!...
BOOM
COME ON, COME ON!
DON'T TAKE THIS LYING DOWN!
AH HA HA HA!
VOOOM
FWMP
THMP
THUD
SKISH
SKISH
SKISH

YOU'RE WORN OUT ALREADY?
BOOORING.
WILL THIS GARBAGE REALLY MAKE ME A LEVEL 6?
WOBBLE...
STAGGER
AH!
NICE. YOU'RE PRETTY TOUGH, HUH?
NOW THAT'S THE SPIRIT!

THERE'S NO ONE HERE...?
O-OF COURSE NOT.
THERE'S NO WAY AN INSANE PROJECT LIKE THAT COULD ACTUALLY EXIST...
KRUNCH
SHUNK

ドシャア
THMP
WHAT'S THE MATTER, HM?
YOU FINALLY DONE FOR?
OR DID YOU JUST DECIDE TO GIVE UP?
KOFF
MISA... KA...
HAS YET... TO ACCURATELY GRASP THE ABILITY OF MISAKA'S TARGET.
HOWEVER...
BASED ON THE EXPERIMENTAL DATA COLLECTED UNTIL NOW, MISAKA SPECULATES... THAT HE THROWS BARRIER-LIKE OBJECTS AROUND HIMSELF.

SEEING MISAKA'S TARGET WALKING WITH HIS FEET ON THE GROUND, MISAKA BELIEVES THAT THE AREA BELOW THE TARGET-- OR THE SOLES OF THE TARGET'S FEET--IS NOT AFFECTED BY HIS ABILITY.
SHF
SHF
MISAKA CONCLUDES THAT AN ASSAULT UPON THE TARGET FROM BENEATH HIS FEET MAY BE MOST EFFECTIVE.
SHF
WHAT THE HELL ARE YOU MUMBLING ABOUT?
IF YOU'RE NOT GONNA RUN, THEN I'M ENDING THIS.
MISAKA WAS NOT RUNNING...
KRAKLE
MISAKA HAS SUCCEEDED IN LURING THE TARGET TO THE PROPER DESTINA-TION.
MISAKA CORRECTS THE ACCUSATION.
ZZKRK
ZZKRK
PI

KA-BOOOOOM
FLASH

FWOOO
TAR-GET... COM-PLETELY ...
SI-LENCED ...?

AGH!
THUD
NOPE! SORRY!!
SQUEEZE!
SQUEEZE!
SQUEEZE!
YOUR DEDUCTIONS WERE WAY OFF THE MARK.
AH!
AH! AH!
TEAR
TEAR
RIP

BZZKRK
UGH!
GAAAAHH!
K-KRAK
TINK

WHUMP
AW, NOW WE CAN'T PLAY CHASE ANYMORE.
SPLUNK
I'M PRETTY SURE YOU'D DIE ON YOUR OWN IF I LEFT YOU HERE LIKE THAT.
BUT IT'S SO *BORING* WAITING FOR YOU TO KICK IT.
!
CLAW
GRAB
PULL

DRAG
SLIDE
SLIDE
PULL
HUH ...?
DRAG
PULL
HEY...
ARE YOU SERIOUSLY TRYING TO RUN AGAIN?
YOU DO KNOW THAT THAT'S A DEAD END OVER THERE.

OR WHAT...? YOU GOT ANOTHER GRAND SCHEME UP YOUR SLEEVE?
DRAG
SLIDE
SLIDE
....
I THINK I'VE HAD ENOUGH OF YOU.
GRIND

I'M GONNA END THIS RIGHT NOW.
?!
NO.
NO WAY!
IT CAN'T BE...

STOP!!
SKY
SQUEEZE

KA-KRUNCH
AND THUS CON-CLUDES...
TODAY'S EXPERI-MENT!!

ER, I KINDA WENT OVER-BOARD THIS TIME...
I WONDER IF THEY'LL BE ABLE TO CLEAN UP THIS MESS.
NOT THAT I REALLY GIVE A DAMN.
CRUNCH
GUESS I'LL STOP BY THE CONVE-NIENCE STORE...
WHUMP
WHUMP
WHUMP
WHUMP
WHUMP
WHUMP
WHUMP
WHUMP
WHUMP
WHUMP
WHUMP

AAAHHHHHHHH!!...
To Be Continued...

GRATZ!! RAILGUN VOLUME 4, YEAH!
I'VE BEEN HONESTLY ENJOYING IT, READING EVERY SINGLE VOLUME! BUT LATELY, TOUMA HASN'T BEEN IN A LOT OF EPISODES, SO PLEASE SUBSTITUTE SOME OF MIKOTO'S APPEARANCES FOR HIM!!
KEJI MIZOGUCHI
I REALLY LOVE ALL THE DIFFERENT EXPRESSIONS FUYUKAWA-SENSEI HAS FOR THE MIKOTOS! NOW IF ONLY THE LAST ORDER WOULD SHOW UP, TOO.
ERETTO

Cheers From the Animation Side (A Congratulatory Message From the Anime Staff)

CONGRATULATIONS ON THE RELEASE OF RAILGUN VOLUME 4. MY NAME IS NAGAI, AND I'VE BEEN GRANTED THE GREAT HONOR OF DIRECTING THE ANIME VERSION. I STILL CAN'T BELIEVE THAT AN OBSCURE PERSON LIKE ME WOULD EVER BE ASKED TO WRITE A COMMENT IN SUCH AN OSTENTATIOUS PLACE...

THE STAFF FOR THE ANIMATED "RAILGUN" AND I WILL TRY OUR VERY, VERY BEST TO MATCH THE AMAZING POWER OF FUYUKAWA-SAN AND KAMACHI-SAN'S WORK!

SO PLEASE BE KIND TO US...

TATSUYUKI NAGAI

PLEASE WATCH THE ANIME, TOO.

2009.10
田中 TANAKA

ILLUSTRATION - YUUICHI TANAKA

And Misaka Was So Looking Forward To It, Too...
AT THE TEA SHOP.
YOU KEEP GOING ON ABOUT "ONEESAMA THIS" AND "ONEESAMA THAT."
DID THEY REALLY TELL YOU THAT MUCH ABOUT ME?
YES.
WE WERE TOLD THAT MISAKA'S ORIGINAL SUBJECT WAS A REFINED YOUNG LADY...
WHO SERVED AS A SHINING EXAMPLE AMONGST THE ELITE OF TOKIWADAI MIDDLE SCHOOL. HOWEVER...
WHAT...?
MISAKA NOW SEES THAT LIFE IS FULL OF DISAP-POINT-MENTS.
SIGH.
WHAT'S THAT SUPPOSED TO MEAN?!
Well, I'm A Sheltered Princess, After All...
SERIOUSLY, YOU LOOK EXACTLY LIKE ME ON THE OUTSIDE.
I DOUBT EVEN MY MOM COULD TELL US APART.
THAT'S NOT TRUE.
MISAKA WILL EXPLAIN.
MISAKA WAS BORN IN AN INDOOR RESEARCH CENTER. MISAKA HAS HAD LESS EXPOSURE TO UV RAYS, THUS MAKING MISAKA'S SKIN MUCH SMOOTHER THAN ONEE-SAMA'S.
ADDITION-ALLY, MISAKA'S HAIR HAS NOT SUFFERED ANY DAMAGE FROM PHOTO-CHEMICAL SMOG.
IN ORDER TO BECOME CLOSER TO THE TRUE ONEESAMA, MISAKA SHALL SEEK TO NEGLECT MISAKA'S HEALTH!!
CLENCH

*In "A Certain Magical Index," Index Librorum Prohibitorum is a silver-haired nun with a bottomless pit for a stomach.

THE HIT ROMANTIC COMEDY ANIME IS NOW A MUST-HAVE MANGA!
Toradora!
© YUYUKO TAKEMIYA / ZEKKYO / ASCII MEDIA WORKS

WWW.ZOOMCOMICS.COM

Alice in the Country of Clover
BLOODY TWINS ~DEE & DUM~
PREVIEW

THIS IS HATTER MANSION IN THE COUNTRY OF HEARTS.
THE HATTER'S ...
JEEZ, THAT MAKES IT SOUNDS SO PEACEFUL.
bloody twins - STAGE: 1.
BUT THEY DON'T MAKE INNOCENT LITTLE HATS HERE.
TAP TAP TAP
DEE!
DUM!
BIG SIS!
THESE TWO ARE THE GATE-KEEPERS OF THE HATTER FAMILY,
TWEEDLE DEE AND TWEEDLE DUM.
AW, WHERE'D YOU GO?!
OOF!
YEAH, BIG SIS!
WE LOOKED EVERY-WHERE FOR YOU!
GAH, WATCH THE AXES!
PUT THEM AWAY BEFORE YOU HUG ME!
GLEAM
OH.
SORRY... WE FORGOT.
WE'LL JUST TURN 'EM INTO GUNS.
ALL SAFE NOW, RIGHT?
FWIP
FWIP
......
LIKE GUNS ARE SO MUCH SAFER.

RUSTLE
RUSTLE
AN INTRUDER!
BANG
WHAT THE HELL ?!
?!
YOU STUPID BRATS!
I'M NOT A DAMN INTRUDER!
AH.
OH.
AND QUIT SHOOTING AT YOUR ALLIES, WILL YOU?
YOUR JOB'S TO SHOOT ENEMIES!
NOW QUIT FOOLING AROUND OR WE'LL DOCK YOUR PAY!
WHA?! DON'T ORDER US AROUND, CHICKEN RABBIT!
YEAH! AN' YOU'RE NOT OUR BOSS-- YOU CAN'T CUT OUR PAY!
THAT'S ELLIOT MARCH.
HE'S A PRETTY DECENT... RABBIT GUY.
THEN MAYBE I CAN PUT A BULLET IN IT!
HE'S GOT A BIT OF A TEMPER.
PUT THAT DOWN, ELLIOT!
SHUT IT, THE LOT OF YOU.
!

BLOOD!
SHALL I KILL THEM FOR YOU?
ER...
NO.
BUT, BLOOD!
SHUT UP, CHICKEN RABBIT!
HE'S ALWAYS WEARING THAT STRANGE HAT.
AND HE'S MOODY AND SELF-INDULGENT.
THE GUY WHO LOOKS LETHARGIC...
IS BLOOD DUPRE.
YOU'RE UPSETTING ALICE.
I JUST WANT EVERYONE TO CALM DOWN!
IN ADDITION...
HE'S THE BOSS OF THE HATTER FAMILY.
THE HATTER "FAMILY."
THEY'RE NOT CONNECTED BY BLOOD...
BUT BY THE BONDS OF THE MAFIA.
WHEN I WAS FIRST THROWN INTO THIS WORLD...
I DIDN'T KNOW ANYONE AND HAD NO PLACE TO LIVE.
WHEN BLOOD TOLD ME I COULD STAY HERE, I TOOK HIM UP ON HIS OFFER.
HOW WAS I SUPPOSED TO KNOW IT WAS A MAFIA COMPOUND?
I WAS SURPRISED...
BUT I DECIDED NOT TO WORRY ABOUT IT.
SINCE THIS IS ALL JUST A DREAM.
SOMEDAY I'LL WAKE UP FROM IT.
HEY.
YOU GUYS...?

LET ME BREATHE.
I CAN'T READ WHILE YOU TWO--
WHAAAT? NO WAY.
YEAH, WE WANNA STICK TO YOU MORE!
BIG SIS...!
D-DO YOU HATE US NOW?!
SWEAT
GULP.
SWEAT
SWEAT
SWEAT
I--
YOU HATE US...?
OF COURSE I DON'T.
UGH.
YAY! WE LOVE YOU, BIG SIS!
I CAN'T WIN.
WHEN THEY'RE ACTING LIKE THIS...
THEY SEEM SO INNO-CENT.
BUT I KNOW BETTER BY NOW
PIT-HOLE
I... I CAN SEE SOME-THING AT THE BOTTOM.
TAG WITH ENEMY SOLDIERS
THEY'RE NOT SWEET LITTLE KIDS.
FAR FROM IT.
HOBBY OF COLLECTING KNIVES

IT'S BEEN A WHILE SINCE I WENT TO TOWN ALONE.
I ENDED UP RUSHING HOME DESPITE MYSELF...
STILL...
I WONDER IF THE BOYS ARE DOING THEIR JOBS FOR ONCE.
TA-DAH!
I BOUGHT SOME OF THOSE DELICIOUS-LOOKING SNACKS I SAW!
I HOPE THEY LIKE THEM.
OH.
THEY ARE WORKING.
THAT'S RARE.
DEE! DUM!
I'M PROUD OF YOU TWO!
AH!
HEY!
WELCOME BACK, BIG SIS!
LOOKIT ALL THE WORK WE DID!
TELL US WHAT GOOD BOYS WE ARE!
YAAAAAAY!
SQUEE!
SQUEE!

!
FREEZE
WE SHOULD STOP, BRO-THER.
TOTALLY, BROTHER.
HUH?
TURN
WE DON'T WANNA GET YOU DIRTY, BIG SIS.
YUP!
WE'LL WASH UP BEFORE TOUCHIN' YOU, 'KAY?
WE'RE GONNA CHANGE REAL QUICK!
PLAY WITH US WHEN WE GET BACK!
HEY, WANNA JUMP IN OUR BATH?!
N-NO, THANK YOU.
IT'S WEIRD.
EVEN TO ME.
THEIR BRUTALITY LIVES UP TO THEIR "BLOODY TWINS" NICKNAME.
BUT EVEN AFTER SEEING IT FIRST-HAND...
PHEW!
THAT FELT GOOD!
SQUEE!
SQUEE!
AND NOW WE'RE CLEAN, SO WE CAN GET GRABBY!
UH, WEL-COME BACK.

...I'M NOT SCARED OF THEM AT ALL.
I CAN'T BELIEVE I LIKE THEM DESPITE THAT.
BIG SIS!
I LOVE YOU. ♥
SMOOCH
H...
HEY ...!
AH! NO FAIR, BROTHER-- LET ME DO ONE!
I LOVE YOU, BIG SIS. ♡
SMOOCH
HEH.
THAT TICKLES.
I LOVE YOU, TOO! ♡
SMOOCH
JEEZ ...
IT'S LIKE PLAYING HOUSE.
MM.
TEA PARTIES REALLY ARE BETTER AT NIGHT.

GOOD.
IT LOOKS LIKE YOU THREE ARE ENJOYING YOURSELVES.
CLIIING
CLIIING
...
YOU SQUIRMY LITTLE SNAKES!
YOU'RE ANNOYING ALICE--LET GO!
PEEL
NO!
YOU SUCK, STUPID RABBIT!
SUCK ME, YOU LITTLE TURDS!
YAP!
YAP!
FREE AT LAST.
PHEW
YOU SURPRISE ME, ALICE.
I DIDN'T REALIZE YOU WERE INTO YOUNGER MEN.
CLATTER
STOP MAKING ME SOUND CREEPY!
I'M NOT "INTO" LITTLE BOYS. I LIKE MY MEN GROWN UP, THANK YOU.
OH?
DOES THAT MEAN I STILL HAVE A CHANCE?
YOU'RE GETTING MY HOPES UP, SWEETHEART.
...!
IT NEVER ENDS.

Continued in *Alice in the Country of Clover: Bloody Twins!*